WITH DR

lefr
6S

-|

Mud and Bodies

Captain Neil Archibald Campbell Weir, Argyll and Sutherland Highlanders.

Mud and Bodies

The War Diaries and Letters of
Captain N. A. C. Weir, 1914–1920

Edited by
Saul David

Preface by
Michael Weir Burns

Frontline Books, London

Mud & Bodies: The War Diaries and Letters of
Captain N. A. C. Weir, 1914–1920
This edition published in 2013 by Frontline Books,
an imprint of Pen & Sword Books Ltd,
47 Church Street, Barnsley, S. Yorkshire, S70 2AS
www.frontline-books.com

ISBN: 978-1-84832-688-0

For more information on our books, please visit
www.frontline-books.com, email info@frontline-books.com
or write to us at the above address.

Printed and bound by CPI Group (UK) Ltd, Croydon, CR0 4YY

Typeset by Donald Sommerville
in 10.2/13 pt ITC Garamond Book and 9.9/13 pt ITC Garamond Light

Contents

—◆—

List of Plates

Glossary

AA&QMG	Assistant Adjutant- and Quartermaster-General, the senior administrative officer in a division
A&SH	Argyll and Sutherland Highlanders
ADC	Aide-de-camp
Adjutant	The commanding officer's right-hand man, responsible for administration, discipline and issuing orders
AG	Adjutant-General; also AAG and DAAG: Assistant and Deputy-Assistant AG, staff officer grades
APM	Assistant Provost Marshal: the officer responsible for a division's internal military discipline
Army	British troop formation of two or more corps, commanded by a general
Battalion	The basic tactical infantry unit of the British Army, consisting of Battalion Headquarters and four Rifle Companies ('A', 'B', 'C' and 'D'), and numbering 30 officers and 1,000 men
BEF	British Expeditionary Force
BF	Bayonet fighting
Billet	Temporary accommodation with civilians
Boche	German (from the French *tête de boche* or obstinate person)
BM	Brigade-Major
Brigade	British troop formation of four infantry battalions (in 1914) and supporting arms (Royal Artillery, Royal Engineers, Royal Signals etc.), commanded by a brigadier-general
BW	Black Watch (Royal Highlanders)
CB	Commander of the Order of the Bath
CCS	Casualty Clearing Station
CIGS	Chief of the Imperial General Staff: the senior officer in the British Army
CMG	Commander of the Order of St Michael and St George
CO	Commanding Officer
Corps	British troop formation of two or more divisions, commanded by a lieutenant-general

Coy	Company
CQMS	Company Quartermaster-Sergeant
CRA	Commander Royal Artillery, the senior artillery officer of a division
CSI	Commander of the Order of the Star of India
CSM	Company Sergeant-Major: the senior NCO in a company
DAC	Divisional Ammunition Column
DADOS	Deputy-Assistant Director of Ordnance Services
DCM	Distinguished Conduct Medal: the second-highest gallantry award (after the VC) for other ranks
Division	British troop formation of three brigades and supporting arms, commanded by a major-general
DLI	Durham Light Infantry
DMO	Director (or Directorate) of Military Operations
DMS	Director of Medical Services
DSO	Distinguished Service Order: the second-highest gallantry award (after the Victoria Cross) for officers
duckboards	Wooden slats used as walkways in the trenches and across muddy ground
dug-out	Underground shelter
DVO	Director of Veterinary Services
FOO	Forward Observation Officer
GOC	General Officer Commanding
'Gooseberry'	Barbed wire entanglement or reel
GS	General Service
GSO	General Staff Officer: concerned with operations, intelligence, training etc. Within a divisional headquarters, the GSO 1 was the principal staff officer. Junior grades were GSO 2 and GSO 3
HLI	Highland Light Infantry
KCB	Knight Commander of the Order of the Bath
KCMG	Knight Commander of the Order of St Michael and St George
KOYLI	King's Own Yorkshire Light Infantry
KRRC	King's Royal Rifle Corps
L/Cpl	Lance-Corporal
LF	Lancashire Fusiliers
MBE	Member of the Order of the British Empire
MC	Military Cross: gallantry award for officers
MM	Military Medal: gallantry award for other ranks
MVO	Member of the Victorian Order
NCO	Non-Commissioned Officer
OC	Officer commanding

OCB	Officer Cadet Battalion
Parados	Mound along the back of a trench to protect against attacks from the rear
Parapet	Protective wall of earth or sandbags at the front of a trench
QM	Quartermaster
QMG	Quartermaster-General; also AQMG and DAQMG, Assistant and Deputy-Assistant QMG, grades of logistics staff officer
RA	Royal Artillery
RAF	Royal Air Force
RAMC	Royal Army Medical Corps
RAOC	Royal Army Ordnance Corps
RAVC	Royal Army Veterinary Corps
RC	Roman Catholic
RE	Royal Engineers
RFA	Royal Field Artillery
RMA	Royal Military Academy, Woolwich
RMC	Royal Military College, Sandhurst
RS	Royal Scots
RSM	Regimental Sergeant-Major: the senior NCO in a battalion
'sausage'	German mortar bomb, shaped like a sausage
SM	Sergeant-Major
SR	Scottish Rifles (Cameronians)
Subaltern	Junior officer
VAD	Voluntary Aid Detachment, a nursing organization
VC	Victoria Cross: the highest gallantry award for all ranks
WAAC	Women's Auxiliary Army Corps
WO	War Office

Preface

By **Michael Weir Burns, grandson of Captain Neil Weir**

I was very young when my granddad died, so I only have a few memories of him. But what I can remember is quite vivid. I was living with my mum, dad and sister in Bristol. As both my parents were teachers, we made the most of our time during school holidays and the long summer break. My grandparents lived just over an hour away, in Holford, a sleepy, rural village set in a combe at the foot of the Quantocks. We would visit them every school holiday as the location was idyllic and the distance not too far.

My grandmother loved the outdoors and would join us for daily walks up the combe and onto the Quantock hills. They had a good-size garden and she would oversee us building makeshift dams in the stream or playing cricket, badminton and so on. My granddad, however, was a totally different character; in fact I have no memory of him ever being outside the house. They lived in a cottage, set into the hill, with small windows, thick walls and low ceilings; it was always warm, but also dark. My granddad used to spend his time at his desk, an elegant oak bureau with a pull-down leaf that could be used as a work area. His study was at the end of the house, down a sloped, well-polished hardwood floor that was great for sliding along in stocking feet. As this was in the 1960s, before most homes had central heating, and there was no shortage of wood where they lived, he would permanently have a real fire going. This gave his study a cosy feel, and the smell of burning wood would fill your nostrils; it would always crackle and spit as if it was alive. I can't remember ever having a conversation with granddad. He would look round, nod his head in acknowledgement and say hello, but not much else. Around his study were several pictures of men in uniform, the crest of the Argyll & Sutherland Highlanders and a few Oxford University college shields. None of this made any sense at the time, but they have much more significance now.

When granddad died in 1967, it had little impact on me. I did not attend the funeral; possibly mum and dad thought my sister and I were too young. Our holidays at the cottage continued as before, and we did much the same thing year after year. The only thing missing was granddad at his desk. My grandmother's death, seven years later, was more memorable as I was then sixteen. The cottage was kept as a holiday retreat, and so began the slow process for my mum and aunt of sorting through my grandparents' belongings. This took a few years: partly because they hated throwing anything away; and partly because there was no hurry as the cottage hadn't been sold. Each time they visited the cottage my mum and auntie would go through items box by box, keeping some things and giving some away, while reminiscing at the same time. Because my granddad had worked for many years for the Colonial Office, a lot of these items were from distant parts of the Empire, and many items were donated to the British Empire and Commonwealth Museum.

Granddad had always been passionate about his family tree. As he had two daughters, it was decided to christen me (the eldest grandson) Michael *Weir* Burns to keep the family name going. So anything that had the Weir family crest, or related to the family, was given to me. Apart from a couple of pieces of furniture, most of this family memorabilia was packed into ten large metal trunks which, over several months, were transferred one by one to our family home in Bristol. At the age of sixteen, these trunks and their contents – mainly papers, books and old clothes – were not of immediate interest to me. I was then a full-time student, working evenings and weekends to make ends meet, and probably the last thing on my mind was to go through some dusty old boxes. But I think I always knew, deep down, that I would eventually find time to go through them properly.

Five years later, I took the trunks with me when I moved into my first house. But because the house needed a lot of work they were put in the loft. This trend continued as the next house I bought was in a similar condition. Then came marriage and children. And all this time the trunks remained unopened. Finally, in January 2009, I had the perfect opportunity to look through them properly: the family home was all but finished, the children were at school and work was ticking over. The trunks were the ones my grandparents had used when they travelled overseas, and granddad had painted big yellow crosses on them to make them easily identifiable. They also had many destination stickers on them, which gave them an antique look. On opening a few of them I discovered old letters, photographs and an army uniform with kilt, spats and sporran. After looking at a few more I unearthed a red book, a little smaller than A4 in size, with the handwritten title:

War Diary, 1914–1920. Personal recollections. Please do not destroy but use can be made of notices for purpose of record. *Neil Weir.*

Intrigued, I opened the diary. Its pages had yellowed over time, but their contents – mainly words but also some hand-drawn maps – held me spell-bound. I could not put the diary down until I'd read it from cover to cover. Until that moment I'd had no idea that my granddad had served as an officer on the Western Front during the First World War. Neither my mum, aunt nor gran had ever mentioned it. And yet here in the diary, on page after page, granddad had written in graphic and, at times, very moving detail about his experiences in the trenches. I kept coming across places and names of famous battles that I recognized, like Vimy Ridge, 'Plug Street', Messines, Loos and the Somme.

After reading the diary a second time, and cross-referencing it with maps, I began to understand granddad's movements up and down the trench line in Belgium and northern France. My next move was to have the diary transcribed into a computer document that I could use to retrace granddad's wartime footsteps. I was not short of travelling companions as many friends were eager to join me. In June 2009, armed with the diary and maps, four of us set off in a car to France. The countryside we drove across was absolutely stunning, and a far cry from the churned-up earth, scattered corpses and shattered villages of my granddad's descriptions. We spent four fantastic days tracing the movement of granddad's unit, and I was so moved by the whole experience that I decided to return to France two weeks later to do it all again, and also to see the places I'd missed on the first trip. I'm incredibly proud of the fact that my granddad commanded a company of Argyll and Sutherland Highlanders (200 men) in the successful attack on the Somme of 14 July 1916, a day Field Marshal Haig would describe at the time as the 'best day we have had this war'. I'm also extremely grateful that my granddad and his contemporaries were prepared to sacrifice their lives to prevent Germany from dominating Europe.

Whenever I spoke of the diary, so enthusiastic was the response that I decided to reproduce it in some way. At first my plan was to produce 100 digital copies for family and friends, but it soon became apparent that 100 was not going to be enough. My next step was to contact a publisher. Fortunately I didn't have to because, by coincidence, a friend of mine mentioned the diary during dinner with a local military historian called Saul David. A couple of days later I received a call from Saul and within a week the wheels were in motion.

I hope you enjoy this book and that you find my granddad's diary as moving as I did. For me it provided a great first-hand insight into what it was like for a young officer to be involved in a mighty all-out war on an industrial scale.

Introduction

It is extremely rare for a cache of First World War diaries and letters as important as the Weir Papers to come to light almost 100 years after the events they describe. They are the property of Mike Burns, a fellow resident of Somerset, who told me over the phone that he possessed not only his grandfather Neil Weir's War Diary – covering the period 1914 to 1920 – but also two large trunks of his grandfather's letters and papers that he had yet to open. I drove round and we opened the trunks together, working our way through a huge pile of correspondence, some of it written in the last two years of the war when Weir was not on active service, and the rest covering his post-war career in the Colonial Office. Apart from the detailed War Diary, written in the 1920s from notes he must have made at the time, we found nothing that covered the almost eighteen months that Weir spent on the Western Front.

Until, that is, Mike spoke to various members of his family who eventually produced more than forty letters that Neil Weir wrote from school, university and the front line from 1908 to 1916. In addition the family produced the diaries of Neil's mother, which in themselves provide a fascinating snapshot of Edwardian upper-middle-class life before and during the First World War; and a large collection of letters written to Neil by his fellow officers and soldiers (many from the front line) after he was invalided out of France towards the end of 1916. Taken together, they chart Neil Weir's remarkable journey from a pampered and naïve public schoolboy to a hard-bitten veteran of the trenches and a staff officer at the War Office who, far from being disillusioned by his experience of combat, was so affected by the comradeship of soldiering that he did everything he could to obtain a regular commission. Having failed, thanks chiefly to red tape and the sharp reduction in the size of the post-war armed forces, he did the next best thing and joined the Colonial Office.

Neil Archibald Campbell Weir was born at his parents' home of 52 Oxford Terrace, Paddington, London, on 25 April 1895. His grandfather, Dr Archibald Weir, had trained as a medic at Glasgow University before moving south to a General Practice in Kidderminster in 1852. He later volunteered for the

Crimean War – where he served as a surgeon on Lord Raglan's Staff and in the hospital at Scutari from January to July 1855 – and finally settled as a GP in Malvern where he remained until his death in 1894. Family legend has it that Queen Victoria herself offered him a knighthood for his work in the Crimea; he turned it down.

Weir's father, also Archibald, was one of Archibald senior's six sons by two wives (there were three wives in total, but the first died childless). He was born on 6 August 1865 at the family home of Link Lodge in Malvern, educated at Charterhouse, and Edinburgh and Paris Universities, and like his father became a doctor, but a surgeon rather than a GP. On 2 September 1891, Archibald junior married Edith Hill, the daughter of M. S. Hill Esquire. They had two children – Neil (the subject of this book) and Edith Dorothy (born in 1899 and known to the family by her second name) – who were brought up in the comfort of a large house in Worcestershire where Archibald was now working as a surgeon.

Every August and September the family spent a three-week summer holiday in popular seaside towns like Worthing in Sussex, Minehead in Somerset, and Woolacombe Bay in Devon. They would stay in boarding houses and hire bathing huts and tents on the beach. In 1906, when he was eleven, Weir went with his mother and sister to Tenby in South Wales. 'Our bronze Wedding Day,' noted Mrs Weir in her diary. 'It is rough luck we have to spend it apart this year. Arch has sent me a sweet letter & the most lovely of little diamond hearts to wear round my neck – it is good of him. I began the day by bathing with Neil & Dorothy at 6:50 a.m., then went to early service to be with my darling in spirit if not in body & renewed my wedding vows. After breakfast Neil & I walked on to Castle Hill & there read books & looked at the view, for it is another glorious day & not so hot.'

On another occasion, while staying at Woolacombe Bay, Dorothy had her bathing dress stolen from a clothes' line where she had hung it to dry. Mrs Weir recorded:

> We secured it in another tent, where two ladies had taken French leave & were undressing to have a bathe. They had evidently tried it on & found it too small & so had flung it away. Such cheek! But imagine their dismay when the owner of the tent came along after they had been in the water & accidentally (ahem!) caught them dressing. I don't think they will easily forget the situation. We shall now have to be more careful with our properties which we have hitherto left down in the tents.

In 1908, at the age of thirteen, Weir was sent to Wellington College in Berkshire. He wrote fairly regularly to his parents and thirteen letters survive. They paint a picture of a popular boy with 'plenty of friends', though he confesses he has more out of his house than in it. He seems to have been an enthusiastic games player and athlete – entering seven races in one sports day – though not particularly talented. Of one inter-house football game, he wrote: 'I did not do much.'

Nor did Weir shine in class, informing his father in one letter that he and another boy were in danger of being sent 'down to a lower form', and in another that he would 'not get my remove'. As Wellington was a college originally set up for the sons of Army officers, its recently-formed Officer Training Corps (OTC)[1] was an important part of school life, with Weir proudly telling his mother that the number in the Corps – 420 – was the 'most of any public school'. The corps offered basic military training for potential officers, though many of its members, possibly Weir among them, had no interest in becoming professional soldiers.

On 18 January 1910, Weir's father died of cancer at the age of fifty-five. It must have been quite a blow to the fourteen-year-old schoolboy who, by default, was now the head of his household. That this death was not entirely a bolt from the blue is clear from Weir's letter from Wellington of 13 March 1909, inquiring: 'How is Daddy? I hope he is progressing . . . If a letter comes for Daddy (from Wellington) don't let him have it until he is home and well. It will be from B. P. [the Head Master] saying Mr Purnell is leaving and that we are going to have a new tutor; but worse than that our old house is going.'

The only positive to come from his father's death is that, for a time, it galvanized Weir to take his studies more seriously. He wrote in an undated letter (that mentions his mother and sister, but not his father): 'I was 12th in my form this week. I hope to get my remove.' The extra effort must have worked because in his final year at Wellington he gained a place to read Classics at Keble College, Oxford.

Weir went up to Keble in the autumn of 1913. In one of his first letters to his mother from Oxford – dated 10 October – he wrote of his college's sporting reputation: 'A man has just been in, asking me to run in a cross country race next Wednesday – no fee. I don't think I shall have the face to join the rugger team, as they are all so good here. The man who plays where I play is a player for Wales. Keble are good at every sport, except rowing.'

Despite his misgivings, he put his name down for the rugby team and 'didn't do anything very wonderful' in the trial. He was also persuaded by his tutor to join the Oxford OTC (of which his tutor was commanding officer),

---

1. The modern OTC was founded in 1908, as part of the Haldane Army reforms, to remedy the critical shortage of officers that had been made apparent during the Anglo-Boer War of 1899–1902. Initially it had a senior division, in eight universities including Oxford, and a junior division, in public schools like Wellington. During the First World War the senior OTCs became officer-producing units and some 30,000 officers passed through them; after the war they reverted to their basic military-training role.

requiring attendance on the odd weekday evening and for a two-week camp in the summer.

Weir enjoyed the social side of university life – informing his mother on 15 October that 'all the Freshers seem so decent and I haven't met a rotter yet' – but he seems to have slipped back into his old lazy ways and did not shine academically. On 26 June 1914, just two days before the assassination of the Austrian Archduke Franz Ferdinand in Sarajevo, the event that would spark the outbreak of the First World War a month later, Weir informed his mother that he had failed his first year's exams. 'It is simply rotten luck,' he wrote, 'as I ploughed in Prose . . . and I did a weak Cicero Trans[lation]. The worst of it is that they didn't give me a chance of redeeming myself, which I think I could have done . . . Now I can't do Mods again until December, so all hope of Honours is gone.'

His studies would soon be far from his mind.

Saul David

Editor's Note

Obvious errors in spelling, grammar or punctuation in the original letters and diaries have been silently corrected, and dates and times, capitalization and some other minor details have been put into standard forms. Editorial commentary appears in this typeface; **extracts from N.A.C. Weir's war diary in this one**; *and letters to and from Captain Weir in this one*.

1.

Service at Home

On 4 August 1914, Britain declared war on Germany, ostensibly to protect Belgian neutrality (which Germany had breached as part of its 'Schlieffen Plan' to invade France via Belgium, in the hope that it could avoid a prolonged war on two fronts). Most of the regular British Army at home was at once sent across to France as part of Field Marshal Sir John French's 150,000-strong British Expeditionary Force (BEF), made up of four infantry divisions and one cavalry division; a further three regular infantry divisions and one cavalry division would soon follow. That left just the Territorial Force of 14 infantry divisions and 14 Yeomanry cavalry brigades in reserve, and to expand the reservoir of manpower that he assumed would be needed to fight a long war, the new Secretary for War, Lord Kitchener, appealed on 8 August for the first 100,000 volunteers.

Kitchener's aim was to raise a series of New Armies, complete in all their branches, with each one replicating the six infantry divisions of the BEF. This was to be done through the normal regular recruiting channels, rather than through the Territorial Force, and the scheme for the first New Army, or new Expeditionary Force as it was originally called, was announced on 12 August. Six of the eight regional commands – the exceptions were Aldershot and the London District – would each provide an infantry division by recruiting at least one 'Service' battalion for every line regiment in their area.

At first the response to Kitchener's iconic 'Your Country Needs You' recruiting poster was slow. But it soon picked up with the daily total rising from 7,000 on 11 August to almost 10,000 a week later, and peaking at 33,000 on 3 September, the highest number of recruits attested on a single day during the whole war. In the first eight weeks, more than 750,000 men between the ages of nineteen and forty had volunteered (Weir among them) to serve for three years or the duration of the war.[1]

On 25 August, Kitchener predicted the army might expand to 30 divisions. By mid-September this estimate had risen to 50 divisions, and to 70 by July

---

1. William Philpott, *Bloody Victory* (Little Brown, 2009), p. 46.

1915, though it would later be adjusted, in April 1916, to 57 divisions overseas and 10 at home.[1] In all there were 30 New Army divisions, divided into 5 armies.

The very first was known as the 9th (Scottish) Division, and it was to a battalion in that formation[2] – the 10th (Service) Battalion, The Argyll & Sutherland Highlanders – that Weir was posted as a newly commissioned temporary second-lieutenant on 26 August. He never mentions why he chose that particular unit, or it chose him; his Scottish heritage must have played its part, though he could just as easily have joined the Highland Light Infantry as it, and not the Argylls, was the local regiment for Glasgow where his grandfather was born.

Like all New Army (or 'Service') battalions, the 10th Argylls was administered and trained by a cadre of regular officers and NCOs who – as Weir confirms in his diary – were resentful at being left behind when their comrades were shipped to France, and who would have looked down on the untrained volunteers and temporary officers as decidedly second-rate. Most of the ordinary soldiers were Scots from in or near the Argylls' regimental depot of Stirling.

The 10th Argylls was raised in August in Stirling, and quickly moved down to Aldershot to begin its training. It was there that 2nd Lieutenant Neil Weir joined the battalion on 20 September, having spent the previous three weeks at an Officers' Training Camp at Churn in Oxfordshire. Like all New Army formations, the 10th was understaffed and underequipped. 'Variously lacking officers, NCOs, uniforms, kit, modern weapons or even the most basic accommodation for the men,' wrote one historian, 'the situation was soon desperate. There was a shortage of specialist personnel of all kinds . . . Any kind of military experience was soon at an absolute premium and many old officers and NCOs were "dug out" and called back to the colours to drill the ranks into some semblance of discipline.'[3]

---

1. In total the British Empire raised 104 infantry divisions by 1918: 12 regular, 1 Royal Naval, 32 Territorial, 30 New Army, 18 Indian and 11 imperial. See Philpott, *Bloody Victory*, p. 44n.
2. In 1914 each infantry division was made of up three brigades, and each brigade of four battalions, twelve in total.
3. Peter Hart, *The Somme* (Cassell, 2005), p. 43.

To **Mrs Edith Weir**[1] *Churn Camp, Didcot*
[Monday] 7 September 1914

Dear Mother,

I hope you are quite well. I think for safety it would be wise to address my letter as:

N. A. C. Weir Esq
10th (Service) Battalion
Argyll and Sutherland Highlanders
Churn Camp
Nr Didcot

There are such tons of letters, and all anyhow, and there are two other camps here besides this one. I hope to get off one week-end.

Yours,
Neil

To **Mrs Edith Weir** *Churn Camp, Didcot*
Saturday [12? September 1914]

My Dear Mother,

Thank you so much for your last letter. Over thirty left to-day to join their regiments, and a great majority have gone away until tomorrow night. To-day we were all inoculated against typhoid, and my left arm is smarting very much from it – as everyone's is.

I have had a letter from M[illegible] and Auntie Bee and a P.C. [postcard] from Uncle. I am glad you are having some good tennis. If possible I shall try and get down for Saturday evening next just to see you, and I should have to start back on Sunday evening to be in here by 10 o'clock. It is now raining hard and is very dreary. I am opening an account at Cox's the Army Bankers, and they will get my pay in for me and also £20 towards kit. I know the kit will be over £20, as everything is so expensive, and in the end I may have to draw on my Savings Bank. We are charged 7/- [7 shillings or 35p] a day and extras here, which I shall pay out of my earnings which amount to about 9/- a day. Tomorrow we have a slack day so I hope it will be fine. Don't forget Berrow's [Berrow's Worcester Journal][2] will you? I hope you and Dorothy are well and you were successful in your exam.

---

1. All of Neil's wartime letters to his mother and sister were sent to the family address of The Cottage, Lower Broadheath, Nr Worcester, where the family had moved after the death of Archibald Weir.
2. The family's local journal, published weekly since 1709, and reputed to be the oldest surviving newspaper in the world.

No time for more.

> *Yours,*
> *Neil*

To **Mrs Edith Weir**   *Churn Camp, Didcot*
                                   Thursday [24 September 1914]

My Dear Mother,

I hope you are quite well. Please excuse me writing on this awful paper, but my note-paper has run out. I hope to come back from here tomorrow (Friday) and I shall travel by train reaching Shrub Hill at 4.41. I shall have my box and a small parcel so could Albert meet me in the trap [and pony] there, or else I will come on to [the next station] by train arriving at 5:33 and stay for tea in Worcester. You need not send an answer about this as I shall do what I have mentioned if Albert is not there. I shall have to join my regiment on Sunday evening or Monday morning. I cannot be quite sure yet if we can go tomorrow (Friday), but if not we shall certainly leave on Saturday and then I should travel by the same train as if I was travelling on Friday.

I will let you know by wire on Friday morning if I am coming. Goodbye.

> *Yours,*
> *Neil*

P.S. I have not heard from you for ages – but I expect you are very busy. We are never told when we are leaving here until a few hours before.

War Diary   Summer/Autumn 1914

It was on [Sunday] the 20th of [September], 1914, that I sailed into Aldershot Railway Station feeling very much like a boy going to his new school. What a feeling! One had a very vague idea as to what the army was really like. Personally I thought that it was an institution where it was necessary to get everything done by brute force, that the senior officers went for the subalterns in the same way that the NCOs went for the men.

But here I was at Aldershot feeling very self-conscious as I stood on the platform in my new uniform while a porter was getting my new valise bag out of the van. Timidly I enquired the way to Talavera Barracks where I had been ordered to report; the porter didn't know. But another man dressed in civilian clothes had heard my question and informed me that he was also on his way to those barracks. Here was luck. I should have a companion to join me when the time came to report. He told me that his name was Knowling. I told him mine was Weir and away we went off together in a cab to Talavera Barracks.

It so happened that Talavera is quite near to the station so we soon alighted at the Officers' Mess, a grim looking building, and it was at the door I met the first Argylls officer I had seen. He told us the way to the Orderly Room where we had to report and he also informed us that he was Mess President. That officer turned out to be Captain A. G. Wauchope. He also kindly told us where the Quartermaster could be found. It was he that allotted us rooms. Here my first introduction to Weller! 'No room for you, young men' said the genial Weller, but it so happened that we were given a room (with Government furniture in) to share.

I think that most of the so-called Government furniture had been pinched by other officers, as there was only a wash-hand stand basin left. So our camp kit came in very useful.

Our next move was to report our arrival. So we went over to the Orderly Room and after a great deal of fuss were ushered into the presence of the second-in-command, Major W. J. B. Tweedie. While he was talking to us, the Colonel, Lieutenant-Colonel A. F. Mackenzie, MVO, entered and here we got our first shock. The Colonel said that at present he had too many officers and that he was afraid that he would have to send us to the 12th Battalion, which was stationed on Salisbury Plain. What a blow. But the Colonel relented and kept us and I was posted to 'A' Company.

The next day I reported on parade to Captain Gordon, the second-in-command of 'A' Company and we marched down to the Baths between the North & South Camps. After breakfast, the whole company turned out under Captain G. W. Muir and went to see some very elementary Field Engineering. That evening I was transferred to 'B' Company (Captain R. J. P. Cox).

Now here I should say that the 10th Battalion was in the first division of Kitchener's Army that was raised. That was the 9th (Scottish) Division. Major-General Sir Charles Fergusson[1] (lately commanding the 5th Regular Division) was in command. The three brigades were the 26th, 27th & 28th Brigades. All were stationed in Aldershot Command.

The 26th Brigade, commanded by Colonel Grogan, consisted of the 8th Black Watch, 7th Seaforth Highlanders, 5th Cameron Highlanders and 8th Gordon Highlanders.

---

1. Later General Sir Charles Fergusson, GCMG, KCB, DSO, MVO (1865–1951). Educated at Eton and Sandhurst, he was a veteran of the Sudan War of 1898 and a former adjutant-general of the Egyptian Army. He would go on to command II and XVII Corps in France, and emulate his father as Governor of New Zealand (1924–30).

The 27th Brigade, commanded by Colonel Scott-Moncrieff, consisted of the 11th Royal Scots, 12th Royal Scots, 6th Royal Scots Fusiliers and 10th Argyll & Sutherland Highlanders.

The 28th Brigade, commanded by Colonel Scrase Dickens, consisted of 9th Scottish Rifles, 6th King's Own Scottish Borderers, 10th Highland Light Infantry & 11th Highland Light Infantry

Our brigade was stationed as follows:– 11th & 12th Royal Scots in Salamanca Barracks, 6th Royal Scots Fusiliers & 10th Argylls in Talavera Barracks.

Most of our senior officers were regular soldiers who had been held back when their battalions had been sent to the front to train our hastily raised mobs. What a prospect for them who had been used to smartness, cleanliness and obedience. The officers and men now working under them had to be taught all these things and with the extra disadvantages of no uniform, no rifles, no training grounds, no band and no recreations.

As already said Lieutenant-Colonel A. F. Mackenzie was in command. The person who chose him for the task of forming the unit knew what he was about. Colonel Mackenzie had only recently left the command of the 3rd Seaforth Highlanders and he had such a personality with officers and men alike that he could get the best out of them. He fired all with his enthusiasm for his regiment, the Argyll & Sutherland Highlanders, and he poured that enthusiasm into our very souls. He was always down on the slacker and waster, but the right man could always feel sure of his help.

The second-in-command was Major W. J. B. Tweedie, a 93rd officer.[1] He was an able and popular assistant.

The Adjutant was Captain W. Glencairn Campbell of the 93rd. I must confess that he gave the impression that he looked down on the temporary officer, perhaps with reason.

'A', 'B', 'C' & 'D' Companies[2] were commanded by Regular officers as follows:– Captain G. W. Muir (93rd), Captain R. J. P. Cox (91st), Captain R. N. Macpherson (Indian Army, 40th Pathans) and Captain G. D. Campbell (40th Pathans). All were ideal for the job.

Captain Cox apparently had the worst reputation as a soldier, at least so I was informed by those who thought they knew. The fact was that he had a great dislike for the slacker, sham and eye-washer; in other words he could be trusted to look after your interests if he knew you were neither.

---

1. In other words he was a regular with the Argyll & Sutherland Highlanders, which itself had been formed from the old 91st and 93rd Highlanders when numbered regiments were replaced by county regiments in 1881.
2. All British battalions at this time were made up of four rifle companies – 'A', 'B', 'C' and 'D', each of around 200 men – and a Battalion Headquarters. Each rifle company was made up of four platoons of around 50 men each.

As a soldier he turned out to be braver by far than any of those who spread these reports. Such is the way of the Army and the world, and I was taken in by these remarks to such an extent that I was in a mortal funk of Captain Cox before I had set eyes on him.

The other officers in 'B' Company were Captain Wauchope, 2nd-in-C; Lieutenant A. Holford Walker (91st), No. 5 Platoon; Lieutenant M. B. Graham (Walter Dunsterille's nephew), No. 6 Platoon; myself as Officer Commanding No. 7 Platoon; and Lieutenant C. L. D. Tully, No. 8 Platoon.

The Regimental Sergeant-Major was RSM Bunnett, a real good man. Our Company Sergeant-Major was CSM Bell, an old gymnastic staff sergeant. My Platoon Sergeant was a Sergeant Smith and the 2nd Sergeant was a Sergeant Grant who shortly afterwards became Band Sergeant of the 11th Battalion and subsequently got a commission in the 9th Scottish Rifles. Our other platoon sergeants were Sergeant Beilby (No. 5), Sergeant Lawrie (No. 6) and Sergeant Duncan McLaughlin (No. 8). McLaughlin eventually did very well and got two Distinguished Conduct Medals. Poor Lawrie was killed at Loos. I cannot remember what happened to Beilby.

Remember that our crowd were without uniforms, but these gradually arrived and we began to look smart.

I cannot say much as to the training but first of all drill on the square, musketry, bayonet fighting etc.

One of my first battalion duties was to take the RC contingent to their church near Cambridge Hospital, and another was to take a crowd of prisoners, absentees and scallywags to Aldershot station to send them off to their rightful places. This was a horrid job as they all got gloriously tight before departing.

To **Mrs Edith Weir**   *Talavera Barracks, Aldershot*
                                         Sunday 4 October 1914

My Dear Mother,

I hope you are quite well. This morning I took all the Roman Catholics of the Battalion to their church in Stanhope Lines – about 250 strong. I am sharing a room with a man called Knowling who lives at Tenby. All the officers here are very nice especially the subalterns. We mess with the Royal Scots Fusiliers, and they are not half as nice as those in our regiment. I am going to be in charge of a platoon in 'B' Company. The whole battalion is quite efficient and our company officers are all regulars. Amongst our officers are Lord Dundas and the author Ian Haig. On Friday (pay day) four of us had to take 67 discharged men down to the station and pay them there. As most of them were dead drunk it was very hard to deal with them. I have met one or two people I know in other regiments, who were at Churn [Camp, near Didcot]. These barracks are situated quite near the centre of the town and station. I don't see much chance of getting a week off yet. We haven't had a spot of rain yet which is lucky.

I sent my money into Cox's yesterday, and have drawn my money from the savings bank. I think we might visit the German prisoners' camp at Frith Hall. Well I must end now as I must write some more letters.

Goodbye.

Yours,
Neil

To Dorothy Weir   *Talavera Barracks, Aldershot*
[Sunday] 4 October 1914

My Dear Dorothy,

Thanks so much for your letter. As to socks any colour and any size will do. Men like them really thick. I don't think anything under 55 pairs would be any good for me, as I should want each man in my platoon to have a pair. Perhaps you can raise these.

With love from
Neil

P.S. The man I share a room with is called Knowling. He knows the S.'s very well.

War Diary   Autumn/October 1914

Then we came on to route marches, and I remember one great occasion in October when the Battalion marched through Aldershot headed by the excellent band and fully kilted. We also started open warfare training on Hungary Hill. During these periods I went through a course of drill on the square and a musketry course at Prince Consort's Library.

The next great thing was to prepare for our musketry course on the Ash Ranges. Our Brigade Musketry Officer, Major Pringle, was a very keen & efficient instructor, but I am afraid he had some trouble with the younger officers.

Our Mess life was a happy one. Everyone felt at home, as the Colonel was never ashamed to sit by the youngest subaltern during meals. We shared the Mess with the 6th Royal Scots Fusiliers, a good crowd. We had our guest nights when our pipers played round the table.

Now as to the changes in the Company, first of all we had the addition of a Company Quartermaster-Sergeant in CQMS Norrie, a fine fellow, who was killed afterwards at Loos.

Tully left No. 8 [Platoon] to take over the Transport, so Laidlaw took his place. Walker got engaged to get married so he was not always available. We had the addition of a Recruits Instructor in Sergeant Logan, mind you, recruits were coming in all the time. Sergeant Hawkins took over Platoon Sergeant of No. 5, but he was not a great success.

To Mrs Edith Weir   *Talavera Barracks, Aldershot*
                                         Monday 23 November 1914

My Dear Mother,

I am sorry I didn't write yesterday. All the men got kilts this week and now look very smart on parade. Today the battalion is being inspected by some Indian Princess, but as I have rather a cold I am not going.

On Saturday the Argylls played the R[oyal] Scots Fusiliers at football. Four of my platoon were playing for the regiment.

We did not go into billets after all this Sunday but we have been spending our time fitting up the Regiment with decent rifles etc.

We are probably billeting next Sunday. I had a photo taken of my platoon on Saturday - I must send you one.

I am sorry to say that some of the men's socks are in a disgraceful condition and full of nothing but holes.

Well cheeroh, I must end now.

                              With love from
                              Neil

To Mrs Edith Weir   *Talavera Barracks, Aldershot*
                                         [Saturday] 28 November 1914

My Dear Mother,

We are off [into] billets tomorrow early - I sent you my new address. You might let relatives know this.

I am sending on Monday from here my box by goods to be paid for at Worcester. Let me know [the] cost of this. Please unpack it - it has been packed here hurriedly. I don't think we shall come back to Talavera. As to Xmas I don't know if I shall get off yet. I hope so.

                              Goodbye.
                              With love from
                              Neil

War Diary   Winter 1914

In November we left Talavera Barracks and Aldershot and went down to some billets in Hampshire so that we could practice more open warfare training.

The 11th and 12th Royal Scots were billeted in the Alton Area and the 6th Royal Scots Fusiliers and ourselves were in the Alresford Area. 'A', 'C' & 'D' Companies were in New and Old Alresford. 'B' Company was at Itchen Stoke about two miles out. Nos. 5 & 6 Platoons were in a farmhouse about 1 mile from the town, while Nos. 7 & 8 were in some barns belonging to Hon. Guy Baring, and very bad billets they were. Our Company Headquarters were in Mr Baring's farm. Laidlaw and I were more than lucky as we were billeted in the rectory [with] the Rev. Vivian Skrine. He and his daughter Miss Skrine did everything they could for our men and ourselves. The little church was used for our Church Parades, the schools were used for a club & entertainment and the rectory was used for men who went sick and for our cookhouses. The people were more than kind and I think the men really realised this. No one groused when we came in late and muddy off parade, as we often did and we always found hot meals and baths awaiting us. Our time was indeed a pleasant one. What with our open training, our sudden air-raid alarms, our concerts, our Christmas & New Year, the period went all too quickly.

To **Mrs Edith Weir**   *Itchen Stoke Rectory, Alresford, Hants*
                                              [Sunday] 6 December 1914

My Dear Mother,

Thank you so much for your last letter. I have plenty to tell you. I am awfully comfortable here at the rectory and the rector is very pleasant. It is about two miles outside Alresford and six from Winchester. There is the vicar's daughter who runs the house – she is very nice. The River Itchen flows just below and the country is very pretty and good for manoeuvring. Two platoons are up here and Capt[ain] Wauchope and I look after them. The vicar has opened the school for the men in the evening where they can smoke and read etc., and we have sing-songs there. Alresford itself is a beastly hole and I don't go there unless necessary.

On Friday we had a route march in pelting rain to Winchester and we visited the 91st,[1] one of our regular battalions which is back from India. Some of the company is lodged with a Mr Baring, who is a brother of Lord Ashburton who lives here. This morning we had a parade service at

---

1. 1st Battalion, The Argyll & Sutherland Highlanders.

the church, all except RCs who would not go. The Presbyterians all came and we crammed the church with our company. The church only holds 120 and is not very artistic. There is another little village called Ovington over the water. The rector is High Church but doesn't wear vestments.

I don't know how long we shall be here but I don't expect for more than six weeks. I don't know about Xmas yet – no one does. I had a letter from Leo Mytrea, but I don't see how I shall get over to see him.

Well cheeroh and please excuse bad writing.

> *With love from*
> *Neil*

P.S. Let Mr Lloyd know where I am and say I have such little time to write.

To Mrs Edith Weir

Aldershot
Sunday 20 December 1914

My Dear Mother,

I am now installed here with the Yorks and Lancs with our recruits who are firing a musketry course at Ash. Five of the Argyll officers are with them and they number 320 strong. I am by rights the senior officer and should have command over the detachment, but as I was sent here a day late, and some other subaltern who is only just my junior was in command, I haven't troubled to relieve him of his post. I have, while I am here, the power of Company Commander and can take Defaulters. The officers of this regiment aren't very nice, although the senior officers are very pleasant. The most extraordinary people are captains and subalterns and I should probably be a full lieutenant in a regiment like this, which is Kitchener's Third Army. We hope to finish this musketry on Christmas Eve if the weather keeps fine. Then we shall get back to Alresford. Send the socks to Alresford, as I hope to be there on Christmas Day. Our Company gets leave on December 28th.

Well I must end now.

> *With love from*
> *Neil*

War Diary

Winter 1914/15

On Christmas Day, the men had a huge lunch in a large barn immediately followed by a big tea given by the Skrines, and after that the officers had their dinner at the rectory, in which the Major in his best jumper was showered with flour.

The New Year we all spent at our homes. Bon.

I must not forget to mention the march we had to Morn Hill, Winchester, where our 91st were in a horrible muddy camp. They went out to France just before Christmas.

Soon after the New Year we were relieved by the 5th Camerons and went back to Aldershot once more.

The men were not sorry to leave their cold and filthy billets, but they were sorry to leave the people and the Skrines.

And so we were back in Aldershot once more, although I personally had been there for a week just before Christmas putting some recruits through their musketry course at Ash Ranges.

And now perhaps I had better give you some idea of the changes made. General Fergusson had left the division and had gone back to France. He was succeeded by Major-General H[ermann] J. S. Landon, CB.

Colonel Scott-Moncrieff had relinquished command of the Brigade to proceed to the Dardanelles. He was followed by Brigadier-General C. D. Bruce. This time we went to Aldershot by road, a distance of twenty-six miles. It was a hot day and a tiring march, but only four men of the Battalion fell out. On entering Aldershot we marched past the General Officer Commanding, General Sir Archibald Hunter, and then took up our abode at Corunna Barracks and again with the 6th Royal Scots Fusiliers.

Although Corunna Barracks were more modern, they were just as uncomfortable as Talavera.

Here we went through another musketry course and became experts in brigade open warfare. I personally went through a machine-gun course under Captain Lumsden, who had taken over the duties of Brigade Machine-Gun Officer. The Battalion were selected as the smartest in the Command to parade before our Japanese Allies, and we went through a lengthy inspection. They could not understand why we wore such funny looking spats. Here I shared rooms with [Sir] Johnnie Dashwood.

At the beginning of February, we left Aldershot once more and marched down to Bramshott Camp, near Liphook, Hampshire. This camp, of course, afterwards became famous as the big Canadian centre but at this time it was unfinished. So much so, that there were no officers' quarters or Mess at all, and the men's huts were in a very leaky condition. The ten weeks here were spent in divisional training, which meant long marches and out for lunches. Divisional training is a somewhat tedious affair for battalion officers, but no doubt extremely interesting to the staffs.

One day I call to mind was when Kitchener, who by the way had inspected us in pouring rain at Aldershot just after the New Year, came down to see the 9th and 14th Divisions fight the 10th, 11th and 12th Divisions near Witley. The whole thing was an awful frost, as the two former divisions never obtained touch with each other, and so we didn't see the enemy at all. All the generals brought out good lunches with them and had a real picnic.

We also went through another musketry course at the Longmoor Ranges and it was owing to this that Graham got pleurisy. Lieutenant S. E. Cameron & Lieutenant J. B. Leask then joined our company. I was sent on a bombing course under the REs [Royal Engineers] at Bordon, and also a range-finding course at Hayling Island.

On return, I left No. 7 Platoon and took over the duties of Bombing & Range-Finding Officer.

The bombing was very primitive. We made our bombs from cut up jam tins, filled with gelignite to which was attached the detonator & fuse. They did not always go off, but a packet of gunpowder went off successfully in my left hand, and made a nasty mess of it. Our chief enjoyment was to blow up the traverses of trenches just near the Mess with guncotton, much to the detriment of the Mess windows. I thoroughly enjoyed the Barr & Stroud range-finder classes, and we got quite proficient in the instrument.

Other excitements included a photograph taken of the officers of the Battalion, and the engagement of Major Cox to Miss Skrine of Itchen Stoke. Consequently Major Cox was not often seen in the Mess. Kenneth Thomson joined our Company with a big car. He took No. 6 Platoon.

Then I must not forget to tell you about the motor bicycle I bought at the garage at Liphook. It was a Douglas and a dud and returned next day to the garage. I had some little trouble with them as it was necessary for me to stop my cheque.

And finally the country round Bramshott was gorgeous even in the spring. Hindhead was quite close to us with its great hill (where German spies were supposed to abound as they signalled to the South coast), the Devil's Punch Bowl was another spot, and let us not forget to mention Haslemere.

The close to our training in England was a fitting one, as we were graciously honoured by a visit and inspection from our Colonel-in-Chief, HRH Princess Louise, Duchess of Argyll.

After the inspection, the officers were all presented, and then HRH took tea with us in the Mess.

After tea I was asked to explain to her the intricacies of the bomb. Naturally I was very nervous (I might not be now) but she seemed to be very interested.

And now the end of April has arrived and we received orders to get ready for France. What an excitement. Officers went to get their heads shaved and looked very unbecoming!

Then came the question as to who was to be left behind with the details. McQueen, Laidlaw, Leask, Thomson & Vitchie were selected, but I was nearly chosen as I still had my arm in a sling. Luckily not.

To **Mrs Edith Weir**

Bramshott Camp, Hampshire
[Friday] 7 May 1915

My Dear Mother,

Thanks for your last letter. I hope you are quite well. We are expecting to leave here soon for France or somewhere else – that of course is a secret to everyone. I will let you know when we are off, as soon as I can.

All my extra kit I am sending on to the Cottage – there will be a kit bag and small wooden box and a bed, wash-hand stand etc.

I should so like you to send me Berrow's and any other interesting papers.

My hand is gradually getting better now and will soon be well.

Goodbye, darling, and I hope you will get over all your troubles soon. Say goodbye to Dorothy and all my friends for me.

With love from
Neil

To **Mrs Edith Weir**

Bramshott Camp, Hampshire
Tuesday 11 May 1915

My Dear Mother,

I enclose the key of my kit-bag.

The last letters, that of yesterday and Friday, I believe it was, should be dated to tomorrow. As to the one written on Sunday seeing that we shall first proceed to the base [sic].

We are leaving tonight, but I am not allowed to tell where for – in fact we don't know ourselves.

I think you will find, somewhere or other, my revolver holster. Would you post this to:

> *J. B. Leask Esq.*
> *10th Argyll & Sutherland Highlanders*
> *Bramshott Camp*

When you get my kit bag, you might take the things out as they will get all crumpled.

I think you know how to address my letters, but in case you don't address as follows:

> *Neil A. C. Weir Esq.*
> *10th Argyll & Sutherland Highlanders*
> *BEF*

Well goodbye, dear, and say goodbye to Dorothy for me, I will write and let you know how I am as soon as possible. My hand is much better now.

With love from
Neil

War Diary   Spring 1915

On the evening of May 10th we left Bramshott Camp and marched to our entraining stations at Liphook. Crowds were there to see us depart, for the Scotch were very popular in Hampshire.

The train came in covered with notices and chalk marks and out it steamed to the tune of Auld Lang Syne.

We reached Folkestone at midnight, and it was in the dark that many looked for the last time at dear old England, the land of their birth.

2.

Service in France

By the time Weir and the rest of the 9th (Scottish) Division were considered ready for service in France in May 1915, the original British Expeditionary Force had all but ceased to exist. It had been blooded in Belgium and northern France at the Battles of Mons and Le Cateau, 23–26 August 1914, fighting two successful holding actions against a much stronger German army and losing more than 10,000 men in the process. It also played a key role in the 'Miracle on the Marne' (6–9 September) when the initial German advance into France was halted east of Paris by an Allied counter-attack that drove the enemy back to the River Aisne where they took up advantageous defensive positions on high ground.

As part of the subsequent 'Race to the Sea', the Germans tried to break through the British salient that had formed in front of the Belgian city of Ypres – the First Battle of Ypres (19 October–22 November 1914) – but little ground was gained and the casualties were huge: the Germans losing 130,000 men, the BEF 58,000, the French 50,000 and the Belgians 20,000.[1] (More than half of the 160,000-strong BEF had by now been killed, wounded or were missing since the start of the war.) Thereafter the opposing sides prepared to sit out the winter by digging trenches that eventually stretched from the Channel coast to Switzerland, with the British holding various sectors from Flanders in Belgium to Artois in northern France.

The first British attempt to break the deadlock was made on 10 March 1915 at Neuve Chapelle, in Artois, when elements of the regular 7th and 8th Divisions (recently assembled from foreign stations) and the Indian Corps (which had arrived in France in October 1914) were given the task of taking the tactically valuable Aubers Ridge. The attack took the German defenders completely by surprise, and within twenty minutes of zero hour a 1,600-yard gap had been opened in the German line. But then the attackers paused to allow their artillery bombardment to 'lift', and this gave the Germans time to bring up their reserves. A later German counter-attack on 12 March by the 6th Bavarian Reserve Division (in which Adolf Hitler took part) was stopped

---

1. David Stevenson, *1914–1918* (Penguin, 2004), p. 76.

in turn with heavy casualties. The final British gain was barely half a mile of ground at a cost of 11,000 men.[1]

The German response was to use chlorine gas to punch a huge hole in the northern sector of the Ypres salient on 22 April (the start of the battle known as Second Ypres). Next day the defenders improvised gas 'masks' by tying cloths soaked in water round their mouths, and the gap was eventually closed by Allied counter-attacks. When the battle ended on 25 May, the salient had shrunk but was still intact.

Meanwhile, further south, a second British attempt to take the Aubers Ridge – in the battle of that name, part of a co-ordinated offensive with the French to pierce the left shoulder of the great German salient from Ypres to Verdun – had been stopped in its tracks on 9 May. A week later, partly to reduce the pressure on the troops at Ypres (where the Germans were still attacking), the British launched the first night assault of the war at Festubert, south of Neuve Chapelle. One of the attacking divisions, the 7th, managed to capture a vital strongpoint known as the Quadrilateral. But all attempts to take the German reserve position failed – partly because the British artillery did not know where it was – and the battle petered out, though small-scale attacks would continue until 27 May. The smell of decomposing bodies was still strong when Weir and his battalion were posted to the Festubert sector in late June 1915.

By then the new British Third Army (made up chiefly of Territorial divisions and the first of the New Army formations, but not the 9th Division which had joined Haig's First Army) had extended its area of operations to near the Somme River to relieve French troops to take part in the failed Champagne offensive. The British now held most of the line from Ypres to the Somme.

War Diary   Spring 1915

The 10th Battalion Argyll & Sutherland Highlanders left England on May 11th under the command of Lieutenant-Colonel A. F. Mackenzie, MVO, as part of the 27th Infantry Brigade (Brigadier-General C. D. Bruce) of the 9th (Scottish) Division (Major-General H. J. S. Landon, CB). We entrained at Liphook Station, near Bramshott Camp and detrained on Folkestone Harbour Station and here we embarked for Boulogne at about midnight.

12 May 1915: We reached Boulogne at about 2:30 a.m. the same morning and marched up to the Rest Camp, where we stayed about seven hours. (Ostrohove).

---

1. John Keegan, *The First World War* (Pimlico, 1998), pp. 208–12.

It was here that I first heard the distant sound of guns coming from a north-easterly direction and it gave one a very sinking feeling in the region of the stomach.

From the camp we marched down to a station about two miles outside the town called Pont de Briques where we picked up the very train on which our transport had come in from Havre, as they had come over via Southampton.

13 May 1915: I cannot say much about my impression of a troop-train, they are certainly 'slow and sure' and eventually, after passing through St-Omer, we detrained at Wizernes, a small town and not very interesting. From here we marched about three miles to our billets.

To Mrs Edith Weir   *Nr. Wizernes, northern France*
                                            Thursday 13 May 1915

Mother dear,

I hope you are quite well. We are now somewhere in France some distance behind the firing line. We had a very good crossing and spent a night at a rest camp and came up into billets here. All the officers in the company are in a farmhouse and the men in various barns. None of the people seem to know a word of English, but our men seem to make them understand what they want. They can get milk and eggs very cheaply. They charge 1d each for eggs which I should think is very cheap. None of us are extra special good at French, but we manage to get what we want. One of our horses did a bunk last night. This news was conveyed by a villager, who was very excited. At present it is raining and not very pleasant. I hope Dorothy is well and don't forget to send Berrow's [Worcester Journal].

With love from
Neil

War Diary   Spring 1915

The Battalion was rather scattered in those billets [near Wizernes]. Our Headquarters and 'A' Company were at Grand Bois, 'B' Company was at Bientques, 'C' Company at Petit Bois and 'D' Company at Pihem. We spent four or five days here and the only interesting thing that happened was when we visited the Machine-Gun School at Wisques, that famous old abbey, which afterwards became the 1st Army School.

16 May 1915: It was on a Sunday just as the company RCs were parading for church that we got our orders to pack up and move. Orders come suddenly on active service, and in this case there was no exception. Part of our new training!

The next part of our active service training was to follow shortly, for we assembled as a brigade, and marched to La Crosse via Arques, where we bivouacked for the night. At dawn next morning we were on the road again, although not before we saw a Zeppelin returning from a raid on the old country.

17 May 1915: We soon picked up the whole Division on the road, and headed for the Steenwerck area via Hazebrouck, Strazeele and Outtersteene.

What a march and the heat was appalling while our Battalion was at the tail end of the Division.

In this area, the Division formed part of the 3rd Army Corps (Major-General W. P. Pulteney, CB).

The Battalion was billeted at La Becque, while Brigade Headquarters were at Noote Boom. Linton got his captaincy and McDonald, Knowling and I got our second stars.[1]

To Mrs Edith Weir

La Becque, northern France
Monday 17 May 1915

Mother Dear,

Just a line to let you know I am quite well. We marched up further today and can now hear the big guns going hard. The march was very hard owing to the cobbled roads and it was pelting with rain the whole time. But now I am in a barn with plenty of holes in it, but it is shelter which is the great thing. It strikes me that some of my letters must take some time to reach you, as a post hasn't gone out for last three days. I have quite a [glut] of Postal Orders as all the men want me to change them into French money. I had my first vision of a Zeppelin today, which was chased by some of our aeroplanes, which rumour has it, was brought down. Well I must close and let me hear from you as often as possible.

With love from
Neil

---

1. Promotion to lieutenant, denoted by two stars or pips worn on the cuff.

War Diary   Spring 1915

19 May: Here [La Becque] we remained for almost a fortnight, during
which time a party of officers (myself included) went up to Armentières
to receive instruction in trench warfare from the 1st Leicestershire
Regiment of the 6th Division, who were in the line just to the east of
town.

To **Mrs Edith Weir**   *Armentières, northern France*
                                                      Wednesday 19 May 1915

Mother Dear,
   *Thank you for letter received today. I am now up in a town only two
or three miles from the firing line. I came up with eleven of our officers
and am going into the trenches tomorrow night on a tour of inspection.*
   *This is a very comfortable billet in a really nice house, only the shells
dropping about in the town make it rather uncomfortable. This morning
when having a drink in a café with some more officers, the Germans
started bombarding and we had to beat a hasty retreat along a street
which seemed to be a favourite spot. Unfortunately the town has been
badly knocked about. Would you believe it that Burberry's have a shop
here, but they charge you through the nose. We shall be in the trenches
for two days and then we return to the Battalion, who are still in the
farms.*
   *Yesterday they discovered a lot of equipment and ammunition in some
ponds nearby, evidently chucked there by someone leaving in a hurry.*
   Well I must end now, also to bed.
                              With love from
                              Neil

War Diary   1915

Armentières has changed since those days. Then it was a respectable
town with shops and hotels and we were billeted near the station in the
Hôtel de la Gare.

   But our instruction was cut short, owing to the fact that the rest of the
Battalion had moved up to the Blue Factory just near the Lys. From here we
moved to the Bois-Grenier trenches through Gris Pot. 'A' & 'C' Companies
were put with the 93rd [2nd Argylls] and 'B' & 'D' Companies to the 1st
Scottish Rifles. My Platoon was attached to 'C' Company (Captain Scott)
of the 1st Scottish Rifles. Our two days were very quiet.

We all caused much amusement to others by the amount of kit we carried. Even blankets were included in the furniture. What heartiness.

To Mrs Edith Weir   *Bois-Grenier Trenches, near Armentières*
                                    10:15 a.m., Friday 21 May 1915

Dear Mother,
I am now writing from the trenches. My platoon is attached to a company who have been here some time and they are learning their job. These are very comfortable trenches and there are jolly good dug-outs in them. There is very little firing in this part of the line, and my platoon is still going strong. Tonight we leave and go back into billets. The town we are billeted in is quite large and has one or two English shops in it, which rook one like anything. The town is quite desolate as it is shelled rather badly.
As we move about a good deal it takes your letters a long time to follow one up and I am surprised that in your last letter you say that you don't hear much from me as I think I have written every day except two. Is Charlie Britten rejoining the Grenadiers when he goes out again?
I suppose you have started tennis or is that suspended due to the war? Well I must end – give my love to Dorothy.
                                    With love from
                                    Neil

War Diary   Spring/Summer 1915

From Armentières we returned to La Becque, but we were soon back again working on trenches at L'Epinette in a disused cemetery, a smelly business. On this occasion we lodged in the Hôtel du Prophète, while the Battalion were in the Station. We worked on these occasions with the 4th King's Royal Rifles.

7 June 1915: Orders again, and at the beginning of June we left the 3rd Corps [of the Second Army] for the 1st Corps (Major-General H. de la P. Gough, CB) [part of First Army]. This meant marching just behind the line to the St-Venant area via Bac-St-Maur, La Gorgue, Robecq, Busnes and Guarbecque, a distance of 36 kilometres. We were billeted on the main road from Guarbecque to St-Venant. Good billets too!
We spent about three weeks in these billets and trained hard. Bombing took up most of the men's time and it was not an easy matter to instruct them owing to the scarcity of materials.

I was Battalion Bombing Officer and had the assistance of these officers:– Ewart 'A', Brownlie 'B', Knowling 'C' and Stevenson 'D'. We also carried out some tactical training in the Bois de Nieppe beyond Haverskerque. [It] shortly fell to our lot to move from St-Venant towards the line via Bourecq (near Lillers), where we spent two nights.

26 June 1915: After a day's hot march we arrived in the Festubert area and were billeted at Gorre, where we relieved the South Staffordshire Regiment in the 7th Division. Divisional Headquarters were at Locon.

30 June 1915: After spending three days at Gorre, presumably as divisional reserve, we moved up to take over the trenches to the east of Festubert and Le Plantin.

Two of our companies, 'A' & 'C', took over the front-line trenches at the small salient called 'The Orchard' which had just previously been taken by the Canadians. 'D' Company was in local support at Piccadilly Circus and 'B' was in the reserve line trenches, nearly 1,200 yards behind the Orchard.

The trenches were in a bad state of repair and they smelt horribly owing to the hot weather and dead Boches lying about.

To Mrs Edith Weir   *Reserve Line Trenches, near Festubert,*
northern France
Sunday 4 July 1915

Dear Mother,

I hope you are quite well. I was up in the trenches yesterday and they are not very grand. The flies and smell are terrible, and seeing that a great many men were killed there not long ago – it is rather unwholesome.

Our men have been out in front of the trenches – that is between the German and English trenches – digging at night. Luckily our part has not been shelled, but they have been shelling a lot. Another thing I have been doing is repairing old bombs. There are plenty up in the trenches. I am trying to hear from you about Uncle C. and where he was buried. We have got a service this afternoon – it is rather impressive with the guns going. By jove, I shall have something to tell you when I get home and I hope if I get wounded I land at [Battenhall?]. I heard from Eliza Harris yesterday – she is in a hospital at Bathieu acting as cook. Well I must go. Love to Dorothy.

With love from
Neil

War Diary   Summer 1915

After four days of a gentle break-in, we were relieved by the 8th Gordons of the 26th Brigade and we marched out into the divisional reserve at La Bohème. Here Holford Walker of 'A' Company left us sick, and Linton of 'D' Company took over a trench mortar squad.

After a week, we moved up to our old place in the line again and 'B' took over the point of the Orchard, with 'C' & 'D' on the right and 'A' in reserve. We relieved the 11th Highland Light Infantry in the 28th Brigade.

This time things were more lively and some interesting patrolling took place along a disused trench leading out from a line in which the Boche were working. Captain Wauchope and Captain Wade both received slight wounds in these adventures. Stevenson was wounded by shrapnel in the back.

To **Mrs Edith Weir**   *Trenches, near Festubert*
                                                 Thursday 22 July 1915

Dear Mother,

Here we are again! And not quite so comfortable as last time as there are no dug-outs and it is very muddy. We got up to our knees last night coming up. I hope you won't mind the stain on the paper but unfortunately something broke in my pack coming up. You can imagine me covered as I am now with mud. My dug-out is 5 ft by 2 and has mud walls. The firing has been fairly heavy so far and I have had little sleep, so I can tell you I am dead tired as we marched about 15 miles yesterday with very heavy packs. Thank Dorothy for her letter – I was sorry she didn't win her tennis tournament.

I don't see any chance for any kind of leave, but there is a rumour that we might get seven days leave after August 11th – hope this is so.

Well dear I must close now hoping you and D. are quite well.
                                With love from
                                Neil

To **Mrs Edith Weir**   *Trenches, near Festubert*
                                                 Saturday 24 July 1915

Dear Mother,

I got Berrow's [Worcester Journal] all right and I am now writing at the unearthly hour of 5:30 a.m. as I am on duty from 2:30–8:00 a.m. – then to bed I go. Things were quiet last night, thank goodness, but yesterday we gave the Allemands plenty of rifle grenades and with success too I

*hope. They of course answered with more grenades but without success.
I got a parcel of groceries this morning and not before it was wanted as
I was getting dead sick of bully beef.*

*I am gradually getting dry but my boots are still wet through, which
they have been the last four days and will be for the next three. The
aeroplanes have been very busy this morning and so have the anti-
aircraft guns who never get anywhere near their mark.*

*I hear from Whitrow – a very interesting epistle. He is still in England
and he tells my old scout[1] at Oxford has been killed at Ypres.*

Well dear, cheeroh.

> With love from
> Neil

War Diary   Summer 1915

28 July: After eight days [in the front line] we were relieved by the 6th
Royal Scots Fusiliers (Colonel Northey) and went into brigade reserve at
Le Touret, a dirty place.

Here Major Tweedie, our second-in-command left us to take over the
9th Argylls, who were then in the Ypres Salient. Major Muir took over
from Major Tweedie and Cavendish took over command of 'A' Company.
As Captain Wauchope went into hospital, Brownlie took over 'B' while
I was definitely posted to Headquarters as Battalion Bombing Officer, a
new Headquarters appointment. Again, after another short tour in the
reserve line trenches, we left for Locon and, finally leaving the Festubert
area, we marched to Gonnehem after spending two nights at Long Coinet
just near Chocques, the 1st Corps Headquarters.

---

1. College employee who acted as a student's servant.

3.

Into Battle

On 7 July 1915, at the first inter-Allied conference of the war at Chantilly (near Paris), it was agreed that all the Allied armies – French, British, Belgian, Serb, Russian and Italian – would keep up the pressure on the Central Powers by launching co-ordinated attacks in the autumn. Lloyd George, Minister of Munitions (since the formation of a coalition government on 26 May), had been keen to delay these attacks until the following spring when more guns and shells would be available. But he bowed to pressure from General Joffre, the French Commander-in-Chief, who was desperate to liberate northern France (which contained most of the country's heavy industry, including its coalfields) from German occupation.

The plan was for the British First Army (including Weir's 9th Division) to attack across the coalfields of Loos, south of Lille, while the French made simultaneous assaults at Vimy Ridge and (their major effort) in Champagne. General Haig, the First Army commander, had wanted to make a second effort at Festubert, to the north, because the ground around Loos was too flat and exposed, with good cover for the defenders in the form of miners' cottages, slagheaps and winding gear. But when the French insisted, Haig gambled all on the first British use of chlorine gas, noting in his diary on the morning of the attack: 'What a risk I must run of gas blowing back upon our dense masses of troops.'[1]

Postponed twice (from the end of August to 8 September, and from then to 25 September), the attack at Loos was against a German defensive system of two lines, three miles wide, with concrete machine-gun posts in between. It was an almost impossible nut to crack, and Sir John French, commanding the BEF, hoped for steady but unspectacular gains. Haig, despite his earlier misgivings, was now more optimistic that his assaulting divisions would make a sufficient breach in the enemy lines for his operational reserve to advance into open country. He was, he told his wife three days before the attack, 'pretty confident of some success' and that by October he hoped the

---

1. Quoted in Gary Sheffield, *The Chief: Douglas Haig and the British Army* (Aurum, 2011), p. 128.

BEF 'may be a good distance on the road to Brussels'.[1] Some of this optimism must have trickled down to regimental officers like Weir who noted in his War Diary 'that it was to be the attack that would end the war, that division after division would break through after we had made the gap in the Boche defenses' and that 'we went into that fight with the firm belief that it was to be the end of Germany'.

The gas was released at 5:30 a.m. and the troops advanced an hour later. In places (particularly where the regular 2nd Division attacked on the right) the gas hung about in no-man's land and even blew back to the British trenches, hindering the advance. The other five British divisions engaged – two regular (1st and 7th), two 'New Army' (Weir's 9th and the 15th Scottish), and one Territorial (the 47th) – had more success, taking the German front line and, in some places, even the second. The 15th Division, for example, captured the first two German positions, the village of Loos and a crucial tactical feature, Hill 70. (Haig would note in his diary: 'The day has been a very satisfactory one. . . We have captured 8,000 yards of German front, and advanced in places 2 miles from our old front line. This is the largest advance made on the Western Front since this kind of warfare started.')[2]

Encouraged, Haig asked French for the operational reserve to join the attack. But these two New Army divisions (21st and 24th) were so far to the rear that they did not reach the original British front line till 6 p.m. on the 25th. When they attacked next day they were cut to pieces, the German defenders standing on the parapets of their trenches to fire into them with rifles and machine guns. Of the 15,000 infantry of the 21st and 24th Divisions who attacked, over 8,000 were killed or wounded. Haig received a report that the divisions were 'running away in great disorder'.[3] The hole left by the 21st and 24th in the British line was eventually plugged by the Guards' Division.

Meanwhile, Weir's untried 9th Scottish Division, which had gained all its objectives during the first morning (including both trench lines, and various strongpoints including the Hohenzollern Redoubt, Fosse 8 and the Quarries), had lost one of them, the Quarries, to a night counter-attack. Haig commented: 'Fine men, and did well in capturing Hohenzollern Redoubt and Fosse 8 on Saturday, but it seems careless to have gone to sleep in a quarry so close to the Enemy!'[4] The Quarries were recaptured by the 7th Division on 26 September, and subsequent counter-attacks against both the Quarries and Fosse 8 at 7 p.m. that day were 'driven back with great loss', noted Haig

---

1. Sheffield, *The Chief,* p. 127.
2. Gary Sheffield and John Bourne (eds.), *Douglas Haig: War Diaries and Letters, 1914– 1918* (Weidenfeld & Nicolson, 2005), p. 155.
3. Quoted in Sheffield, *The Chief,* p. 129.
4. Sheffield and Bourne (eds.), *Douglas Haig,* p. 157.

in his diary.[1] Fosse 8 was lost to a German counter-attack a day later, shortly before the 9th Division was relieved by the 28th Division.

As Bombing Officer, Weir's task was to follow up the initial assault and use bombs to clear the enemy dug-outs. Yet, as he explains in his diary, he was delayed by casualties and enemy prisoners-of-war clogging up the communication trench to the front line, and did not go 'over the top' until 90 minutes after the first troops. He got as far as the Quarries, but was told he was too far to the right and eventually found the remnants of his battalion and a scattering of others units, under a Colonel Dundas of the 11th Royal Scots (part of the same 27th Brigade), in a communication trench called Fosse Alley, a 'dreadful place [with] no parapet or firing step'.

His battalion was relieved that night by troops of the 24th Division as the Germans were counter-attacking the Quarries (an action which led to the capture of 27th Brigade's commander, C. D. Bruce), and on returning to the British front line Weir took over 'B' Company from the wounded Captain McPherson.

By the evening of the following day, 26 September, Weir and his battalion were back in Fosse Alley with the 6th Royal Scots Fusiliers on their right and some of the 9th Royal Sussex (of 24th Division) on their left. Twice on 27 September they beat off German attacks but, with both flanks exposed, and almost out of ammunition, they were ordered to withdraw to the next trench (the old German support line). It was during this phase of the battle, as the neighbouring 26th Brigade tried to counter-attack, that the divisional commander, General Thesiger, was killed (one of three major-generals to die at Loos). Shortly after this the 9th Division was relieved and taken out of the line. Weir commented in his diary: 'What a show. Few instructions, little ammunition or bombs, next to no support from the artillery. No system of looking after the wounded. And practically no food. No wonder we lost the ground we had won and lost so many in casualties.' Weir was one of just nine unwounded officers in the battalion. His 'B' Company was left with 25 effectives.

Attack and counter-attack continued at Loos for another day, but any chance of a comprehensive victory had vanished. The French operations in Champagne and Artois had also failed, and Joffre temporarily halted the offensive. It was renewed at Loos on 13/14 October; but in spite of some careful preparations, the attack on the Hohenzollern Redoubt failed, and Haig blamed the commander of the 46th (North Midland) Division, Major-General Hon. E. J. Montagu-Stuart-Wortley, for using up his reserves 'before they were really required'.[2]

---

1. Ibid.
2. Ibid., p. 164.

The battle had gained for the BEF nothing more than a narrow salient two miles deep, and had cost 16,000 British soldiers their lives with a further 25,000 wounded. Total German casualties were 25,000.[1]

Back in Britain, meanwhile, on the day Weir went 'over the top' for the first time at Loos, his mother and sister were enjoying a 'beautiful morning & perfect Italian sky' on holiday in Minehead, Somerset. His mother noted in her diary:

> We took the Lynton coach as far as Horner Wood & thus made the ascent to Cloutsham, the scene of the Devon & Somerset Staghounds' meet. There were many on horseback & foot & a good sprinkling of motor cars & char-a-bancs. We were very fortunate in seeing the "tufters" find three stag & the pack laid on & away.

War Diary   August 1915

16 August 1915: At Gonnehem we trained and it was here that I first saw Sir Douglas Haig [commanding First Army] riding through the village. French got a poisoned knee and left us. Tully, the Transport Officer was given his captaincy, and Brownlie his second star [lieutenancy].

19 August 1915: During our stay here we were inspected by Lord Kitchener at Busnes. I took temporary command of 'B' Company on this occasion. Just after that I was granted special leave and on arriving back found that the Battalion had gone up to trenches in the Vermelles area, just opposite the Hohenzollern Redoubt [near Loos]. The Transport was at Beuvry and Divisional Headquarters were at Sailly-Labourse.

There had been one or two changes. Major-General Thesiger, CMG, had taken over command of the Division from General Landon. There were also fixed reliefs of trenches and we interchanged with the 8th Gordons, whose second-in-command was Major R. P. Cox, our old Company Commander in England. Meanwhile Captain McMillan had taken over 'B' Company, which however he soon handed over to Captain McPherson, who had commanded 'C' since Aldershot days. Beith was appointed Assistant Adjutant (a new appointment) and Jack Christison with John Dashwood ran the machine-gun section. When we were in billets, we lived in the Rue de Frederick George in Béthune.

Béthune, although rather too far from the line, was certainly the place to live. There was plenty of amusement and the Shell Café and Hotel in the Square were fine places. The theatre was also in full swing, and the 2nd Division concert party gave some fine shows.

---

1. Keegan, *The First World War*, p. 218.

Our reliefs with the Gordons worked very smoothly and while up in the line we were watching the Boche by patrolling and preparing for the coming [Loos] offensive by sapping out into no-man's land and digging new trenches well forward. It was in doing this that Colville of 'D' Company was badly wounded in the hand, although not before he had earned the first Military Cross given to the Battalion. Company Sergeant-Major Norrie, our old Company Quartermaster-Sergeant, who was now Command Sergeant-Major, was killed by machine-gun fire and was one of the first men to be buried in that huge cemetery at Vermelles.

To **Mrs Edith Weir** *Transport Billets, near Vermelles*
Monday 30 August 1915

My Dear Mother,

I have got home [to the 10th Argylls] quite safely after a long journey. To start the train from Shrub Hill was ½ an hour late and I nearly missed the connection at Oxford and would have if that train had also not been late.

I met Uncle Harry at the station and then went on to the [illegible] where we had a talk. He wants to hear more from you after you have seen Uncle Herbert. I caught the leave train from Victoria – by hat! It is a sight to see it go off as there are crowds of people cheering. We had quite a good voyage although rough – I was on the deck the whole time. I got to our railhead at 5:45 a.m. to learn that our Battalion was in the trenches, and to get to our transport it was eight miles. Luckily a cart met me and now after sorting my kit I sit down to write to you. It appears we are next to our 2nd Battalion and the trenches are seven miles off yet. The Battalion went in last night so everything is settling down today. I believe the German trenches are 900 yds from us, but they send those beastly aerial torpedoes,[1] which cause tremendous damage. You don't know how I enjoyed my holiday mother dear and I am looking forward to another. Colonel is on leave now.

Goodbye.

Yours
Neil

P.S. The billets the transport are in are in such a pretty village about the size of Omburdsley.

---

1. British military slang for a type of large trench mortar bomb with prominent fins.

War Diary Summer/Autumn 1915

28 August 1915: While on the line, my chief job was to supervise the provision of bomb stores and prepare sketch maps of the trench system, which was an extremely complicated one.

In billets my bombing sections, of which there were five, prepared the Battye Bombs[1] for the [forthcoming Loos] offensive. I think we put together 2,000 and packed them ready in their boxes.

This is perhaps where I should mention that in that part of the world were the great minefields of France. Each coal mine could be easily distinguished by its various slag heaps. For the rest, the country was flat and dotted with mining villages with typical miner's cottages. Thus it was considered an easy spot for an offensive, as the various objectives were so clearly defined.

But what did the average regimental officer know about this coming attack? Only this:- that it was to be the attack that would end the war, that division after division would break through after we had made the gap in the Boche defences.

And we went into that fight with the firm belief that it was to be the end of Germany.

As it stood that was perfectly all okay and that information warmed us up, but how much better it would have been if we had known our limitations, our objectives, our trenches and the country in front of us. We hadn't even a decent trench map.

To Mrs Edith Weir *Billets in Béthune*
Thursday 23 September 1915

My Dear Mother,

We are to the trenches again soon and this time I shall not have much time for writing, so the field post card will have to be used.

I am going to the theatre again tonight – oh no I am not extravagant as it is only 5d a time. I have just got a letter from George Weir and he seems quite well – I have also received some papers from the Lloyds.

Well dear cheeroh.

> *Yours*
> *Neil*

---

1. An early grenade designed by Captain B. C. Battye of the Royal Engineers. It consisted of a cast-iron mug, diced for fragmentation, and filled with 40 grammes of high explosive. The bomb was sealed by a wooden stopper and lit by a Bickford safety fuze. It was soon superseded by the safer and more effective pineapple-shaped Mills bomb.

War Diary Autumn 1915

The four days previous to the 'show' we were in billets at Béthune putting on the finishing touches. On the evening of September 24th, the Battalion marched up via Beuvry to Annequin, a well-known mining village. Just to the east of Annequin we got into our assembly trenches. I remember quite well that we nearly started off with casualties in doing this. One of my bombers, who was carrying a box of ten grenades, dropped them on the ground and one went off.

We didn't get much sleep that night, everybody felt too windy. But we knew that the 27th Brigade was in Divisional Reserve and the 10th Argyll & Sutherland Highlanders were in the Brigade Reserve.

25 September 1915: At 5:30 a.m. our bombardment began and we slowly moved up Scottish Trench, one of the long communication trenches. The battalion bombers brought up the rear of the Battalion, while the machine gunners under Beith were just in front. Moving up we passed through the lines of guns, all making a deafening din. But how slow our progress was! When should we reach the Central Boyau, the last lap of communication trench? The trenches were absolutely blocked. Stretchers were coming down from the front, although they should have used the 'Down' Barfs [*sic*] Alley trenches. Boche prisoners were also hindering our progress. And then to crown it all, one of the other battalions in the Brigade, cut our Battalion in two.

Thus when the machine gunners and bombers got over the top, we were one and a half hours behind the first company in the Battalion.

Once in the open things went better. We extended in a line and advanced in rushes as we were under fire from the top of the Hohenzollern Redoubt, although our infantry had passed beyond the place. I remember chucking my water bottle to the first man that I had ever seen dying.

Eventually the bombers reached the Quarries, and I found out from a Colonel in the Queen's that we were a little too far to our right. However the 7th Division had apparently lost touch with the 9th Division. On we moved, bearing to our left and came into nasty machine-gun fire from the direction of Cité St-Elie. This place had also apparently been neglected by the infantry of the 7th Division. In order to avoid this fire we took refuge in a trench called Fosse Alley, and found the rest of the Battalion.

Fosse Alley was a dreadful place. It was really a Boche communication trench with no parapet or firing step. Here we discovered that, although our infantry had gone ahead, the right of Fosse Alley was held by the Boche. The Gordons even got as far as Haisnes, but from here the line bent back to pit No. 8 and Cité St-Elie.

Night came on and we still held Fosse Alley. 'We' doesn't mean the Argylls but a mixture of all units under command of Colonel Dundas of the 11th Royal Scots. No news had been received from Brigade Headquarters and everybody was in the dark.

Up to date the casualties amongst the bombers had not been very severe but as soon as we arrived at Fosse Alley, my sergeant, Sergeant Wilson of 'A' Company, was shot through the heart.

We heard that Captain Campbell of 'D' Company had been killed, and that Captain McPherson of 'B' Company had been wounded badly in the ankle. McPherson insisted on carrying on until ordered back by one of the Brigade Staff. Cavendish of 'A' Company was wounded as was also Ewart. Cameron and Ardill of 'B' Company had also been wounded.

At about 9:00 p.m. a tremendous firing commenced in our right rear. It transpired that the Boche had attacked the 7th Division in the Quarries and that they were working round to take us in the back. This, coupled with the fact that we were being relieved by units of the 24th Division, put everybody into confusion. Luckily the Boche did not get much further and we got back to our original front line unmolested.

It was in this attack on the Quarries that our Brigadier, Brigadier-General C. D. Bruce, was taken prisoner and his Brigade-Major, Major Buckham, was killed.

On getting back to our original front line, we foraged for food and I received orders to take over 'B' Company.

Thus ended the first day of the battle [of Loos].

26 September 1915: On the morning of the second day we tried to re-organise and gather together those who had been scattered about the night before, during the hasty relief.

As I have said units of the 24th Division relieved our Brigade and they were now holding Fosse Alley and the east side of Fosse No. 8.

Towards midday our sentries reported that they saw masses of our troops retiring towards our trench (the original front line). What had happened was that some of the newly tried troops of the 24th Division had been unable to withstand the counter-attacks of the Boche. However, apparently the situation was retrieved as we were not called out to assist.

Meanwhile Knowling had taken over 'A' Company and McDonald 'D' Company, while I had 'B' and McMillan still commanded 'C'. Brown of my Company had gone down the line sick.

At about 5:00 p.m. we got orders to prepare ourselves for a night working party and we were all dished out with shovels etc. We started to move off at about 8:00 p.m. under guides from the front line. We moved through the Hohenzollern Redoubt and up [a trench called] Little Willie.

Unfortunately just as we were getting out of this place, the Boche started his antics and commenced another counter-attack, while we came in for the barrage. One of his shells landed in amongst my small Company, and laid out some of the men, at the same time blinding McDonald and myself. When we came to our proper senses the men had moved on and we were left alone with about half a dozen men. Our small party continued to move, but, unknown to ourselves, in the wrong direction and we bore off to our left and came in for some machine-gun fire. Luckily we discovered a wounded officer of the Black Watch and he told us that we were on the left side of Little Willie.

The number of wounded along that trench was appalling. Apparently the Royal Army Medical Corps orderlies had not been out to collect. We also discovered some wounded Boche officers in a dug-out guarded by wounded Camerons. We eventually got back to our starting point, and after more wanderings discovered the Battalion working in Fosse Alley again. No other troops were there and how long the place had been empty I don't know. The 6th Royal Scots Fusiliers were on our right, their right flank was exposed and some of the 9th Royal Sussex of the 24th Division were on our left holding the trenches in the front of the Fosse.

Thus ended the second day.

27 September 1915: The dawn of the third day saw us putting in some useful spade work, but we didn't have peace for long. You must remember that we had originally started out on a fatigue party, but now we found ourselves in the possession of trenches in the front line.

At about 6 o'clock the Boche put in an appearance from the direction of Haisnes and he made a frontal attack without much success thanks to Beith's machine guns. He also started to bomb the Scots Fusiliers on their right and he gradually forced them out of the trench. Then he made another frontal attack, but was beaten off again. But by this time we had no grenades and little rifle and machine-gun ammunition.

Then he got in on the left of the Royal Sussex and, after a short fight, they withdrew leaving our left flank exposed and out right flank in a very shaky condition. Finally he got on the Fosse and took us in the back. It was here that McDonald in a gallant effort to protect our flank was killed. It was a sad loss as he had a great power of organising resistance.

At this point Colonel McKenzie and Colonel Northey gave us the order to retire back onto the next trench (the old Boche support line). It couldn't be helped; we had no ammunition left. This withdrawal cost us many of those who were left. I was in luck and landed in among the 11th Royal Scots absolutely dead beat. I soon found Bonnyman, Knowling and Christison and we gathered a few men together. Colonel McKenzie had been badly wounded in the hip and was carried in by Pte. McFadden of my company who showed the utmost bravery by carrying five or six wounded. He only got the Distinguished Conduct Medal for this.

Moving down the trenches towards the right, we came in for another battle. This time the 26th Brigade were counter-attacking and driving the Boche back. It was here that Major-General Thesiger, our divisional commander, was killed.

Finally we were ordered to get back to our old Headquarters and there we found Major Muir and Captain Campbell. Collecting the remnants we staggered down to our old assembly line at Annequin where we got some food and slept.

Thus ended the third day.

28 September 1915: The next day we walked to Béthune and put up in our old billets and tried to collect ourselves. On our way we passed the 93rd and I especially remember seeing Alistair Campbell.

What a show. Few instructions, little ammunition or bombs, next to no support from the artillery. No system of looking after the wounded. And practically no food.

No wonder we lost the ground we had won and lost so many in casualties. As far as I can remember these were the officers left: Major Muir, Captain Campbell, Lieutenants Beith, Christison, Linton, Dashwood, Bonnyman, Knowling and myself. And the men, I only had about 25 left in 'B' Company.

Well at Béthune we rested, and incidentally found that all our kits had been wetted through. We got together and tried to discover those who were absent or missing.

The next day [29 September 1915] we got orders to entrain at Fouquereuil, one of the suburbs of Béthune, for an unknown destination.

To **Mrs Edith Weir**

Northern France
Thursday 30 September 1915

My Dear Mother,

I take the very first opportunity I have of writing to say I am safe and well after all the ordeal of the last week about which you have probably read in the papers. I cannot say how things went, except that our Regiment distinguished itself above everything and now all our Division has been taken out for a rest a long way behind the firing line.

I hope at some future date to tell you more about it but this is all I can write for the present.

I lost a great part of my kit and should like you to send out my cardigan.
I got your letters from Minehead. Let everyone know I am well.
Love to Dorothy.

> *With love from*
> *Neil*

4.

The Ypres Salient

Sir Douglas Haig's grand hopes for the Loos battle had been dashed; but it was his chief, Field Marshal Sir John French, who lost his job. Blamed for taking too long to release the operational reserve by his subordinates (including Haig), by King George V (a friend of Haig's and undoubtedly biased in his favour), and, ultimately, by the government, French was replaced by Haig as Commander-in-Chief of the BEF on 19 December. Haig saw Loos as a 'great opportunity missed . . . all we wanted was some Reserves at hand to reap the fruits of victory and open the road for our Cavalry to gallop through!' French was, he believed, 'solely to blame for the mishandling of the reserves'.[1] Tellingly he also felt that the battles of 1915 had exhausted the Germans, and was optimistic about the future. This politicking in the high commands, far removed from the front, was in stark contrast to the 'mud and bodies', the grim ordeal of daily life, that Weir and others experienced in the trenches.

After Loos, the 9th (Scottish) Division was given just a couple of days rest before it was sent back into the line in the reduced Ypres salient, first in trenches near Hill 60 above the Ypres–Comines Canal, and then further north in the infamous Sanctuary Wood, 'at the very point of the salient' where the trenches were 'at this time the nearest to Berlin'. The routine was four days in the trenches, four days in huts at Dickebusch a few miles to the rear. For Weir even the rest days were an ordeal. 'It was a record year for mud [at Dickebusch] and you were knee-deep everywhere you walked. The men could not keep clean and life was a perfect hell.'

The only respite from the mud was at Poperinghe, a town seven miles to the rear, where Weir and his fellow officers used to ride for 'a bath' and a performance of the 6th Division theatre troupe known as the 'Fancies'. It was also the location of the famous Talbot House, or 'Toc H' as it was known in signalese, a soldiers' rest home that had been founded by Neville Talbot, senior chaplain of 6th Division, in memory of his fallen brother Gilbert. 'Toc H' provided a sanctuary for men of all ranks to drink tea, read newspapers and, if they desired, pray in the 'Upper' Room. It survives in Poperinghe to this day.

---

1. Quoted in Sheffield, *The Chief*, pp. 131–2.

War Diary

The train journey from Fouquereuil did not take very long, even for travelling in France and after passing through Lillers and Hazebrouck, we detrained at the small country station of Abeele on the Belgian frontier. From here we marched to Reninghelst and on entering the village marched past our old divisional commander, Sir Charles Fergusson.

Here we stayed for two days, during which time we washed up and received a visit from the 2nd Army Commander, General H. C. O. Plumer,[1] and our new Divisional Commander, Major-General W. T. Furse.[2]

From what we gathered from their talk to us, it was generally considered that we had done well at Loos, but that we should get no rest as it was necessary to send us up straight to the trenches in the Ypres Sector.

Shortly after Linton went sick and Dashwood took over his Company. Major Muir also had to go to hospital, so the Battalion was taken over by Major W. G. Campbell with Christison as Adjutant. Tully acted as second-in-command. The company commanders were as follows:– 'A' Company – Captain F. J. D. Knowling, 'B' Company – myself, 'C' Company – Lieutenant W. S. Stevenson, 'D' Company – Lieutenant Sir J. L. Dashwood.

The command of the 27th Brigade was taken over by Brigadier-General H. E. Walshe, CMG. Major N. Teacher was appointed Brigade-Major, while the Hon. W. Fraser became Staff Captain.

Three new officers were attached to my Company, Lieutenant R. Thomson, 2nd Lieutenants A. D. Duff and C. H. Dickerson, all of the 13th Battalion. Sergeant McLachlan acted as Company Sergeant-Major, Sergeant Aitken was acting Company Quartermaster-Sergeant.

Captain J. H. Beith, who eventually got the Military Cross for his work at Loos, also left us to take over the duties of Brigade Machine-Gun Officer and to assist one of our old officers, Captain W. V. Lumsden.

---

1. Later Field Marshal Viscount Plumer (1857–1933). Educated at Eton, and a veteran of colonial warfare against the Sudanese, the Matabele and the Boers, Plumer is regarded as one of the better British generals of the First World War. A meticulous planner, his finest hour was Second Army's capture of the Messines Ridge in June 1917. After the war he became High Commissioner for the British Mandate of Palestine.
2. Later Lieutenant-General Sir William ('Windy Bill') Furse, KCB, KCMG, DSO (1865–1953). Commissioned into the Royal Artillery in 1884, Furse served as an aide-de-camp to Lord Roberts (1891–3) and in the Anglo-Boer War of 1899–1902 as a staff officer at Army Headquarters. He left the 9th Division in December 1916 to become Master-General of the Ordnance and retired in 1920.

To Mrs Edith Weir   *Reningbelst, Ypres Sector*
                                         Saturday 2 October 1915

My Dear Mother,

I hope you and Dorothy are quite well. We are now in Belgium so you see we are north a bit. You can get things much cheaper here which is one blessing and the Flemish more or less speak English. Cigarettes are not so expensive. However the billets are not so good here and we chiefly have to live in huts which are now rather cold. This reminds me of one or two small needs in the way of clothing. If you could possibly send out my 'flea-bag' it would be so useful and also a woollen scarf (khaki) and a pair of light 'gym' shoes or indoor shoes. I should like my gum-boots [Wellingtons] and a pair of Oxford shoes too.

I am writing to Uncle George as I must see him now.

By George – the cold was awful last night, but it is boiling hot today. Our men are getting re-fitted and also are having baths today. There is a YMCA in the village who dispense various luxuries.

We hope to get a post today, the first for a week, so I expect it will be a large one.

Well no more at present. A bath towel would also be useful.

                    With love from
                    Neil

War Diary   October 1915

After two nights at Reninghelst, we moved on to Canada Huts at that horrible place Dickebusch and bivouacked there for the night. I think it was this that finished off Major Muir who had been feeling ill for some time. Early next day the company commanders went forward to reconnoitre the trenches just south of the Ypres–Comines Canal. These trenches were numbered 27 and 28, while the trenches to the north of the canal at that famous spot, the Bluff, were numbered 29.

The 17th Division as part of the 5th Corps (General Allenby) held this line as far as Sanctuary Wood some three miles further north. On their right the 14th Division held the Messines Sector.

The Battalion soon followed the company commanders up and we relieved the right of the 17th Division. 'C' Company looked after 27, 'A' Company took 28, 'B' Company were in support to these two companies while 'D' Company was in reserve on the Canal Bank. I shared a dug-out with Stevenson.

As our companies were only about fifty strong, we received companies from the East Surreys of the 24th Division, who had followed us up from

Loos. This was really their period of trench instruction.

Shortly after 'A' Company moved over to Trench 29 (The Bluff) and 'B' Company took their place in Trench 28. It was at this time that my East Surrey company were expecting a relief, [and] left my front line without orders. Luckily their relief, consisting of Argyll drafts, arrived soon after.

Two days later 'B' Company and 'C' Company were relived from trench 27 & 28 and we went down to the canal dug-outs to hold strongpoints behind the Bluff.

Part of 'C' Company were actually holding the front line with 'A' Company.

Soon after this one of the most disastrous affairs in the whole history of the Battalion took place. At early dawn the Boche discharged a huge mine underneath the Bluff.

Luckily 'A' Company had few killed, but the percentage of wounded and missing was high. Knowling, the Company Commander, acted in a very cool and brave way during the crisis and was eventually awarded the Military Cross.

The next night we were relieved by the Royal West Kents of the 24th Division and we went back to Dickebusch Huts. Company Sergeant-Major Gilchrist now became my Company Sergeant-Major. After three days so-called rest we moved up to the Hill 60 Sector. Passing Crump Corner near the canal, we came in for bad shelling.

The Battalion was in support and 'B' Company was scattered in redoubts round Bedford House, where the Battalion Headquarters were. 'C' & 'D' Companies were in support to the 11th Royal Scots. 'A' Company were left back on the Ypres high road.

Shortly after 'B' Company moved up to Trench 47S right opposite Hill 60. 'D' Company took over the trench to the right (3 November 1915).

Trench 47S was the worst trench I was in during my stay in France. To start off, there was water knee-high and no proper parapet. Parados there was none and only one tumble-down dug-out for Company Headquarters it was also hard to maintain touch with the companies on our right and left. During our brief stay here for three days, we had twenty-six casualties and the 7th Seaforths who relieved us, lost most of their officers. Sausages[1] and bombs were plentiful.

We then marched to Dickebusch again through Zillebeke.

During our stay at Dickebusch, Sergeant Brodie became my Company Quartermaster-Sergeant. He remained in this position until the end of the war – almost a record.

---

1. A German mortar bomb shaped like a sausage.

To **Mrs Edith Weir**   *Dickebusch, Ypres Sector*
                                        Saturday 30 October 1915

My Dear Mother,

I got your letter dated October 25th. It is all right about my income tax as I get it back through my bankers. By the way, I have been appointed a temporary captain or rather I should say a temporary temporary captain, which means if anyone comes out senior to me I revert again to lieutenant. The great thing is the pay which now reaches about 16/- a day (with allowances). We go up to the fire trench again soon and this time in a most unhealthy spot.

I am rather anxious to know if you got my cheque as I have heard no word about it from you yet - you might let me know if you got it.

Goodbye.

                            With love from
                            Neil

War Diary   November 1915

Our next duty was to relieve the 3rd Division in Sanctuary Wood. The wood was at the very point of the salient and the trenches here were at this time the nearest to Berlin.

The Battalion had three companies in the front line and one in reserve. Battalion Headquarters were at the western edge of the wood. There was also one battalion of the Brigade on our right, one in support in Maple Copse Wood. The fourth battalion was in reserve at Dickebusch Huts. On our left was the 17th Division.

The Battalion dispositions were as follows:- 'D' Company were on the right, 'C' Company were in the centre and 'B' Company in B4 on the left 'A' Company were in reserve. 'C' Company's frontage was very wet, but 'B' Company's front was full of mining activity and its left was in the air.

We carried on in these positions until December 18th, interchanging every four days with the 11th Royal Scots. During our periods out we spent the time at Dickebusch. It is doubtful whether these periods can be called 'rest'. It was a record year for mud at the place and you were knee-deep everywhere you walked. The men could not keep clean and life was a perfect hell.

The little recreation we got was a ride to Poperinghe where one could get a bath and see a performance of the 'Fancies', the 6th Division party. On one occasion, I rode into Poperinghe with Stevenson and we were both togged up in our cleanest uniform. Just as we were reaching the railway crossing, Stevenson's nag shied and he came off, covering his new tunic with mud.

To **Mrs Edith Weir**

My Dear Mother,

Just a line to hope you are quite well. I hear we shan't get our full rest, but are going back to the trenches again. It is bad luck - we are awfully sick about it. I went into a town [Poperinghe] about seven miles from here and bought some clothes. I am just back - so no time for more.
                    With love from
                    Neil

War Diary   November–December 1915

Well, let me get back to the trenches. Mining activity was our chief foe. On one occasion our miners had a hand-to-hand fight with the Boche just under my trenches. There was also considerable activity in the 'Birdcage' a fortified post in the Boche line. Consequently there was plenty of patrolling. The Boche also had a daily strafe with shelling and trench mortars. It was during one of these unpleasant episodes that my friend Jack Christison, who was adjutant, was shot in the head by a sniper, as he was standing next to me (2 December 1915). He never recovered consciousness and he died in the field ambulance and was buried in Vlamertinghe Churchyard. Such a gallant fellow and a real loss to the Regiment.

We had a good many changes amongst the officers during this period. Captain N. McQueen and Captain Ian Stewart took over command of 'C' & 'D' Companies respectively. Stevenson succeeded Christison as Adjutant, while John Dashwood and Bonnyman ran the machine gunners.

Leggett was still Bombing Officer and Tully was still Transport Officer. Lieutenant-Colonel H. P. Burn, DSO, of the Gordon Highlanders came to take over command, so Major W. G. Campbell went back to second-in-command.

Regimental Sergeant-Major Bunnett was killed by a shell in Maple Copse and was succeeded by CSM Eadie. Bunnett was a great loss. He had been Regimental Sergeant-Major since the formation of the Battalion.

Amongst the Company drafts, we were lucky to see Sergeant Logan back. Let me mention here that the four best days the Company spent were in some dug-outs in the bank of the Ypres–Comines Canal. I think we were sent here for a treat, as we were apparently forgotten by the Brigade Staff and so had no working parties to perform.

My officers were all fit. Duff did some exceptionally good patrolling. Towards the middle of December we were told that we were to be relieved by the 50th Division and the Durham Light Infantry was to actually relieve our unit. Unfortunately the Boche made a gas attack on the 6th Corps on our right and we came in for some very heavy shelling on December 19th to 24th.

The gas attack was a complete failure so the Boche wreaked his vengeance on our trenches. We were in the centre company at the time and all our trenches were blown in. When the 8th Durhams relieved us on December 21st there really were no trenches left.

After being relieved in the front line we waited six hours in support and then marched or rather doubled out of the Salient via Zillebeke and along the Ypres Railway through Ypres itself to Vlamertinghe where a train was waiting to take us to Bailleul.

We were gas shelled the whole way down, a distance of about ten miles. It was the worst relief I have had.

On arriving at Bailleul we detrained and marched out to Outtersteene to brush and wash up and spend a Merry Christmas.

To **Mrs Edith Weir**

Outtersteene
Tuesday 21 December 1915

My Dear Mother,

Just a line to let you know I have arrived safely in rest billets, for a month too, I believe. We had an awful time this last time in the trenches, and were shelled all day. I can now disclose where we have been since [Vermelles] – in the Ypres Salient. We were in trenches at Hill 60, and Sanctuary Wood, and my trench was the nearest in our line to Berlin. The Boches gassed us on Sunday and gave all the roads a nasty gas shelling, so we are well out of it. Last night when all the transport was moving they were badly shelled, so all those Woodbines – every one – were lost. It is rotten luck.

Well Mother I must switch off – hoping D. is well.

With love from
Neil

Top: A selection of Neil Weir's memorabilia, including clothing from Wellington School and Keble College, Oxford, and his Argyll and Sutherland Highlanders' uniform.

Above: Six out of the ten metal trunks packed with Weir's papers and artefacts.

Above: One of the metal trunks filled with Weir's letters.

Right: Saul David looking at a selection of Weir's war letters.

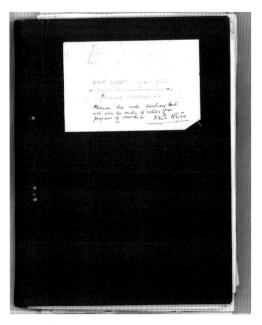

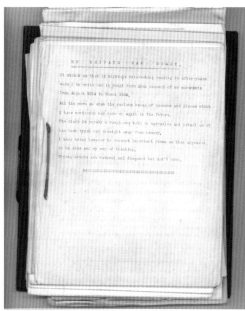

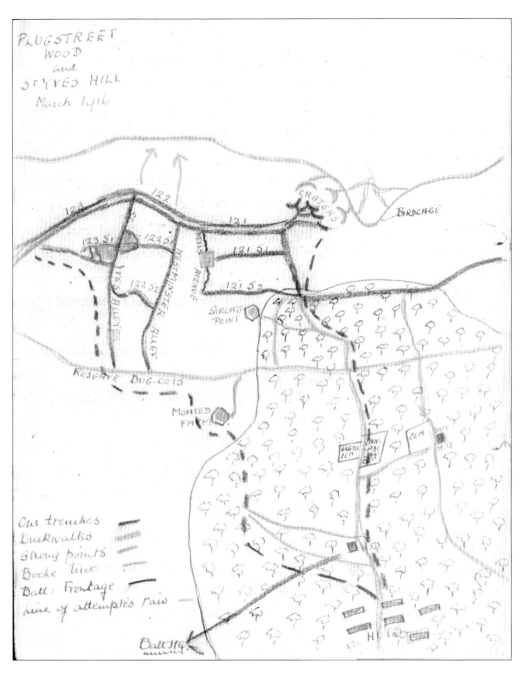

Above: Weir's original map of 'Plugstreet' where he fought alongside Winston Churchill in 1916.

Top left: Front cover and introduction page of Weir's diary.

Left: Weir's roll book which lists each of his men, their qualifications and military role.

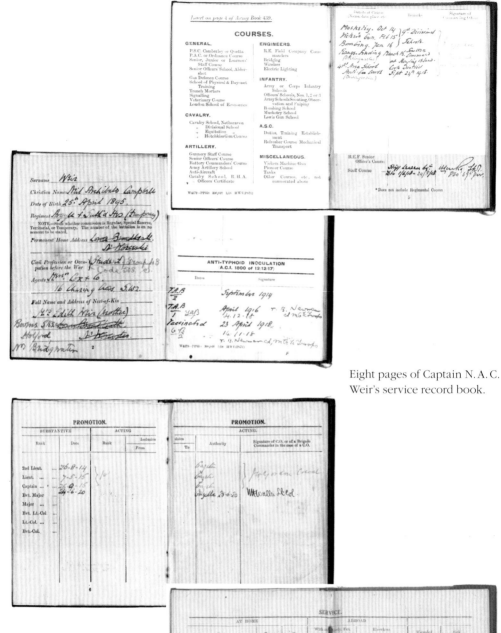

Eight pages of Captain N. A. C. Weir's service record book.

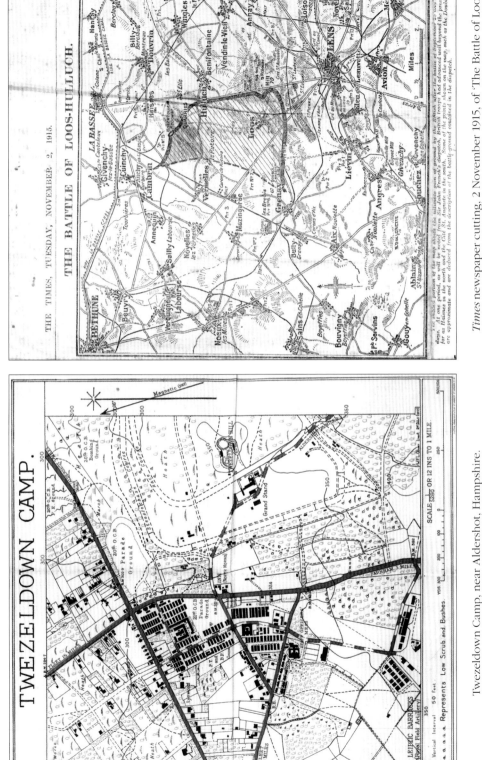

Times newspaper cutting, 2 November 1915, of 'The Battle of Loos'.

Twezeldown Camp, near Aldershot, Hampshire.

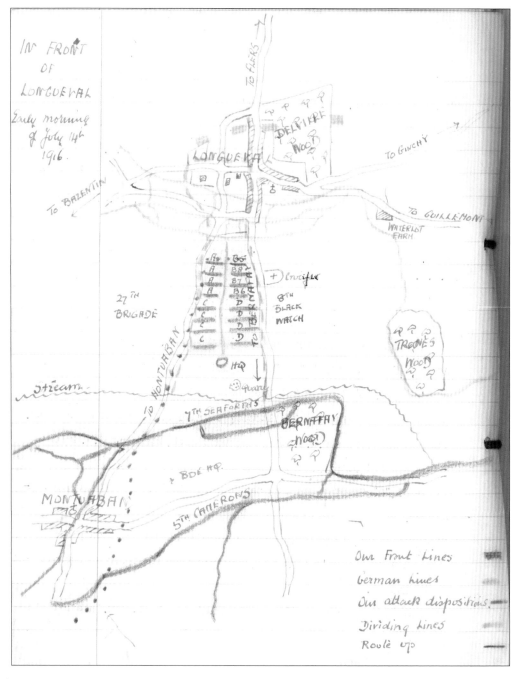

Weir's war diary map showing the no-man's land 'jumping-off' positions for the
14 July 1916 attack on Longueval.

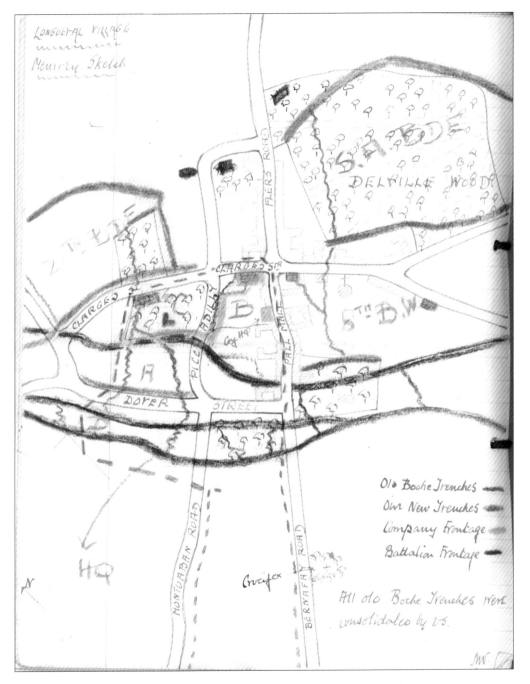

Weir's map of positions after the capture of Longueval on 14 July 1916. General Haig described this achievement as 'the best day we have had this war'.

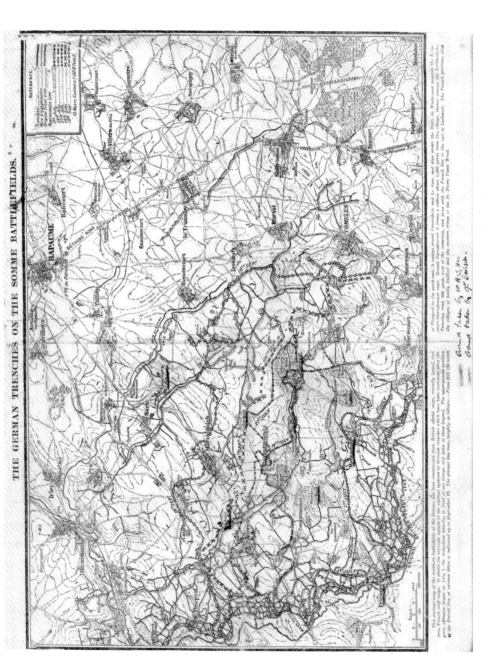

A newspaper map of the Somme annotated by Weir to show ground taken by 10th Argylls (in pink) and by 9th Division (in blue).

To Mrs Edith Weir   *Outtersteene*
                                    Saturday 25 December 1915

My Dear Mother,
    *We are going strong, but the men are really keeping their Xmas [until]
the [New] Year. They won't have a bad feed with plum puddings, apples,
oranges, dates, beer and cigarettes! We shall have our little bust tonight.
Two roosters, plum pudding, fruit and fizz. I will drink your health all
right. We have got a football match this afternoon - Officers v. Men. I am
not playing but shall go for a ride instead. I hope you have a good dinner
at the Marriotts - mind you do.*
    *We got no mail yesterday but I hear there is a large one today. Well
dear I must close now. Goodbye.*
                          With love from
                          Neil

5.

'Plug Street'

In the New Year, 1916, the 9th Division moved to a new area of operations in and around the infamous Ploegsteert Wood – 'Plug Street Wood' in Tommy slang – just to the south of the Ypres salient. It was from here that twenty-year-old Lieutenant Roland Leighton had written to his fiancée, the future author Vera Brittain, in April 1915. He had, she noted in her diary, 'found the body of a dead British soldier hidden in the undergrowth a few yards from the path. He must have been shot there during the wood fighting in the early part of the war. The body had sunk down into the marshy ground so that only the tops of the boots stuck up above the soil.'[1] (Leighton was shot and killed in December 1915).

In autumn 1915, shortly before Weir's arrival, another young officer described the conditions at Plug Street Wood as 'appalling'. He added:

> We have had about three days continuous rain, and the result is the trenches are flooded and the country round is a sea of mud ankle-deep, and in some places today I have been over my knees in it. I took 150 men to do drainage work under the R.E.s on the communication trenches on the left of where we were before we came out. It was an endless, hopeless task. The walls had caved in in places, and as soon as the muck was cleared out it caved in again, and it all had to be done again.[2]

The spontaneous 'Christmas truce' of 1914 – when soldiers had met up in no-man's land to sing songs, exchange souvenirs and even, in one instance, play football – was not repeated a year later. 'Nothing of the kind is to be allowed on the Divisional front this year,' one British infantry brigade was informed. And yet in the front line close to Plug Street Wood 'a tremendous voice entertained the trenches of both sides with a selection from *La Traviata*, stopping abruptly in mid-aria as if a door had been slammed shut'.[3]

---

1. Quoted in Martin Gilbert, *First World War* (HarperCollins, 1995), p. 144.
2. Quoted in Richard Holmes, *Tommy* (Harper Perennial, 2005), p. 247.
3. Quoted in Lyn Macdonald, *1915* (Penguinl, 1997), p. 592.

On 8 January 1916, prior to moving into the Plug Street Wood trenches, Weir informed his mother that the 'next' battalion was commanded by none other than Winston Churchill MP, a fact he saw as 'curious'. He was not wrong. Three days earlier, and just six weeks after his resignation from the War Cabinet as Chancellor of the Duchy of Lancaster, the 41-year-old Churchill had taken command of the 6th Battalion, Royal Scots Fusiliers, at Méteren, near Bailleul, with the rank of lieutenant-colonel. He was an eccentric if popular commanding officer who restored morale after the horrors of Loos, serving with the battalion alongside Weir's 10th Argylls in the front line.

On one occasion, going up to the trenches, Churchill watched shells land ever closer:

> One could calculate more or less where the next one would come [he informed his wife], and I said, 'the next one will hit the [ruined] convent'. Sure enough just as we got abreast of it, the shell arrived with a screech and a roar and tremendous bang and showers of bricks and clouds of smoke and all the soldiers jumped and scurried . . . It did not make me jump a bit – not a pulse quickened. I do not mind noise as some very brave people do. But I felt – twenty yards more to the left and no more tangles to unravel, no more anxieties to face, no more hatreds and injustice to encounter . . . a good ending to a chequered life, a final gift – unvalued – to an ungrateful country.[1]

Fortunately for Britain, Churchill survived this narrow scrape, and many more, before his brief period of active service ended on 6 May 1916 when the depleted 6th and 7th Battalions of the Royal Scots Fusiliers were amalgamated into a single unit and the more senior colonel of the 7th Battalion took precedence. Churchill returned to government as the Minister of Munitions in July 1917.

War Diary   January 1916

On leaving the Ypres Sector, we left General Allenby's 5th Corps and on entering the Bailleul district we came into the 2nd Army Corps which was commanded by Lieutenant-General [Sir] Charles Fergusson.

We arrived at Bailleul at about 4 a.m. very tired and weary. From here we marched out as a Battalion to billets between Méteren and Outtersteene. 'B' Company were billeted in two farms and Company Headquarters were at the farm Hogenacker. All the billets were very scattered, but quite nice. During the five weeks we spent here, we had our Christmas and New Year festivities. I was away on leave at the New Year.

---

1. Quoted in Gilbert, *First World War*, p. 225.

To **Mrs Edith Weir**   *Bailleul District*
                                                          8 January 1916

My Dear Mother,

I arrived all right this morning [back from leave in England] and found plenty of letters for me, including one from Mr Whatley and one from Mr Attwood, in which the former says he had paid £75 into my account. I couldn't get the typewriter after fagging all over the place for it. Winston Churchill is now commanding our next Battalion - which is curious. We had bath parade this morning in great style.

Cheeroh.

                                        Yours,
                                        Neil

War Diary   January–March 1916

We were inspected by General Plumer, the 2nd Army Commander, and General Fergusson. Most of the time we spent in practising Bombing, machine gun work and sniping. Lieutenant Colvin was in charge of the sniping.

The Division Grenade School was also re-opened at Outtersteene and we were all supposed to qualify for the 1st Class Grenadier Test.

All 'B' Company passed with the exception of four men.

Another novelty was the 1st edition of the Battalion paper 'The Argyll Pink-un'. This paper aimed at making complimentary remarks about companies and persons.

There were few changes in the Company, but Lieutenant R. Thomson left for the Machine Gun [Corps] and Lieutenant J. Kennedy took his place. Divisional Headquarters were at Merris.

Then we moved up to the Plugstreet Wood Area to relieve the 25th Division, spending one night in a small hamlet just north of La Becque. Leaving early next morning we moved up to the shell area and were put in Brigade Reserve at the piggeries. Piggeries they were sure enough and we were unfortunate to have a fatal Lewis Gun accident during our two days stay here (28 January 1916).

The Battalion took over trenches just to the east of the wood at the Birdcage (another one) running up to St-Yves Hill where our left flank rested. The trenches were numbered 121, 122 and 123. 'B' Company were on the right guarding the Craters, 'D' Company were in the centre and 'A' Company on the left in touch with the 12th Royal Scots. 'C' Company was in reserve. Perhaps I should now describe my first impression of 'Plugstreet Wood'.

It must be remembered that the 4th Division fought a bloody battle in the wood in 1914 and they succeeded in reaching the east of the wood and managed to consolidate. In this they were assisted by the 19th Brigade and so our 2nd Battalion had fought there.

When we first saw the village of 'Plugstreet' it was practically intact. The Boche rarely shelled it owing to the number of spies living in it. The wood itself was thick except near the east side, where the trees had been blown away by shell fire.

The chief feature was that there were no communication trenches through the wood and only very inferior ones leading up to St-Yves. Thus one was continually exposed to the view of the Boche. Even some of the strongpoints behind our front trenches could be seen by them. There were also no support trenches to speak of, so that it was an easy matter for the Boche to attack and beat us back. On the other hand his trenches were strongly fortified and from our various observation posts on St-Yves Hill, we could see him at work strengthening them. The trenches were on an average 200 yards apart, except near the Craters where they were only 30 or 40 yards away.

The Craters were quite enough trouble in themselves, as they were only held by posts with next to no protection. Just opposite them was the Birdcage a very well fortified strongpoint forming a salient in the German lines.

Thus there was plenty of work to be done on the trenches as well as exceptional vigilance.

After seven days in the line we were relieved by the 7th Seaforths and in all 'B' Company did three tours in Trench 121.

During this time we worked like niggers and put the Craters into some state of defence by filling them in with wire. It was found to be very difficult to wire outside the Craters so we chucked 'Gooseberries' over the top.

We also put our main trench into some state of repair and started to rebuild the parapets also building the parados.

Our tours out we spent at the hutments at Rabot, where there were decent baths and we could always get into Armentières. It wasn't very pleasant for the men as they were continually going up to the line on working parties.

There was a good canteen at Romarin, where entertainments and cinema shows were given. I remember Lena Ashwell's party coming with their baby piano.

Day by day the Boche were getting more objectionable. No doubt this was brought on by the trench raids which had just been inaugurated. However he shelled 'Plugstreet' village badly until it was impassible by day. He also shelled the various farms where the different headquarters were. Even Divisional Headquarters had to leave Nieppe for Steenwerck, while Brigade Headquarters had two or three changes. Winston Churchill came in for a bad time too; he was commanding our sister battalion, the 6th Royal Scots Fusiliers.

St-Yves Hill trenches were always being knocked in and all the strong-points were badly shelled.

'Moated Grange' the largest one, was leveled. The Boche also had a nasty trick of firing with indirect machine-gun fire into the wood at night and one had to lie flat on one's face on the duck-walks when this occurred. Colvin, our Sniping Officer, was wounded in this way.

Our artillery were especially good at retaliating. In fact the liaison between ourselves and the artillery was improving every day. Captain Hon. O'Stanley worked in conjunction with my Company.

During this period, Brigadier-General Walshe relinquished his command of the Brigade and was succeeded by Brigadier-General G. F. Trotter of the Grenadier Guards. Major W. G. Campbell also left for the staff and his place was taken by Major J. C. Scott, DSO. Captain H. G. Sotheby, MVO, also joined, taking command of 'A' Company from Knowling. Both these officers had served with the 93rd.

Our third tour in Trench 121 opposite the Craters was a little more lively. Certainly we had got on with the repair of the trenches and the Boche knew that too. In fact he knew the names of the companies opposite him.

When we heard him talking too loudly we threw a few bombs into his craters and certainly on one occasion spoilt his rations. He of course retaliated and so we had one or two casualties.

Apropos our artillery liaison, our 18-pounders often had strafes and on one or two occasions popped their shells into our trench. I used to telephone down in alarm and Stanley [the artillery liaison officer] would come running up in order to tell me not to be a fool.

Our telephone system was none too good. In fact the Boche seemed to hear all our conversation on the phone and incidentally we could hear his. Hush. Hush. What about our mining under the Birdcage? We were suppose to have the largest mine on the Western Front in this sector of trench. This caused us considerable anxiety as many thought that the Boche would raid and attempt to destroy it. Our staff were always developing schemes to protect it and Windy Bill, General Furse, and his GSO 1, Colonel (afterwards Brigadier-General) S. E. Holland, were always up in our trench. It was about this time that Colonel Holland left and Colonel P. A. V. Stewart, King's Own Scottish Borderers, took over the duties of GSO 1.

'B' Company's next tour was in support in Hunter's Avenue. We also had platoons in the various strongpoints including Moated Far.

During these periods we worked like slaves and the various communication trenches leading along St-Yves, Westminster Avenue, Wells Avenue, 121 S1, 122 S2 and 123 S2 & S4 soon began to look as though they were trenches. We also started a new breastwork through the wood. No. 8 Platoon was particularly expert at putting up the new U-shaped frames.

'D' Company, commanded by Ian Stewart, made a raid on the Boche lines opposite Trench 122. Unfortunately the affair was a failure and 2nd Lieutenant Matheson was found to be missing. There were also fourteen other casualties including Ian Stewart himself. Captain. C. C. G. Johnstone of the 93rd took over command of this company.

To Mrs Edith Weir   *Ploegsteert Sector*
                                                         13 April 1916

My Dear Mother,

Thank you very much for your letter and Berrow's [Worcester Journal] of last night.

I am afraid leave is knocked on the line, as all leave is stopped. I can't even get special leave on business grounds.

I am not quite sure what ought to be done about handing over on April 25th [Weir's 21st birthday when he would have received his inheritance]. I heard from Attwood yesterday and he said I must make a Will etc!

I was wondering if you could help me by going over to Whatley [the family solicitor] and interviewing him, getting him to draft me a Will in favour of you and Dorothy.

Also the trustees have the deeds to hand over and I was wondering who had better keep them for me. What about Sheppard?

I am writing to Attwood and Whatley about it – so Cheeroh.

                                                         From
                                                         Neil

War Diary   April 1916

A little later Lieutenant-Colonel H. P. Burn left us and our new Colonel was Colonel W. J. B. Tweedie, our old second-in-command. It will be remembered that he originally left us to take command of the 9th Argyll and Sutherland Highlanders. Bonnyman also gave up the machine guns and went to the Division as Claims Officer. His job was taken on by Lieutenant R. W. Davidson.

Further changes were in store. On the South African Brigade joining the 9th Division, it was necessary to get rid of four battalions. Consequently the 6th Royal Scots Fusiliers (Winston's Battalion), 8th Gordons, 10th & 11th Highland Light Infantry went to the 15th [Scottish] Division, while we went to the 26th Brigade and 9th Scottish Rifles & 6th King's Own Scottish Borderers went to the 27th Brigade. Brigadier-General A. B. Ritchie was in command of the 26th Brigade with Major Drew as Brigade-Major and Captain J. C. Simpson as Staff Captain. The command of the 27th Brigade was taken by General Scrase Dickens in place of General Trotter, who had a bad fall from his horse. General Lukin was in command of the South African Brigade.

It was at this time I again proceeded on leave.

To Mrs Edith Weir   *Pullman Car Service, Continental Express,*
South Eastern and Chatham Railway
12 May 1916

My Dear Mother,

Just a line as I am travelling down to Folkestone – so please excuse the writing. I saw Uncle Hugh last night and had drinks with him and Uncle Harry[1] *at the [Caledonian] Club [St James's Square, London] – they were both very jovial. Afterwards Uncle Harry and I went to the Prince of Wales's [Theatre] and saw 'Mr Manhattan' – a very good piece indeed with, of course, lots of beauties in it. We didn't get back until 12 midnight so I am pretty tired today, as this train started this morning at 7:50 a.m.*

Well I had a jolly good time at home – I only wish it had been longer. Uncle Hugh cannot tell when he can get down and see you as he is very busy, and when Uncle Harry gets away he will have to go to Liverpool first.

With love,
Neil

War Diary   May–June 1916

On my return [from leave in mid-May] 'B' Company had just taken over Trench 122, the centre company. Nothing of note happened during this time as far as the Boche were concerned. We had the South Africans up

---

1. Hugh Heywood Weir (born 1875) and Henry Bright Weir (born 1880) were the sons of Archibald Weir senior and his third wife Anna-Marie (née Bright), the niece of Dr Richard Bright, Queen Victoria's personal physician. Both were educated at Harrow and Trinity College, Cambridge.

for Trench instruction and Captain Burn Murdoch, the Adjutant of the 14th Battalion, also spent one or two days with the Company.

Lieutenant A. D. Duff, who had been with me since October, left for a trench mortar course at the 2nd Army School. Unfortunately he lost his right arm through an accident and so never came back. 2nd Lieutenant Ramsay and 2nd Lieutenant McLardy joined the Company. Claude Tully also gave up the Transport and went as APM [Assistant Provost Marshal] of the 24th Division. Dick Knowling took his place.

Our next tours were still further to the left in Trench 123. It was during this time that the winds were very favourable for Boche gas attacks. However he didn't trouble us but the 11th Royal Scots, who were holding the trenches at the edge of the wood, were heavily raided. Soon after we had men of the 41st Division up for trench instruction and we were relieved by the Royal West Kent Regiment of that Division. The Boche of course knew all about the relief, so that we couldn't use the wood at all.

We then went back to Rabot (or Papot) for one night, our last night in the Ploegsteert Area. What a change. 'Plugstreet' was a haven of rest when we arrived in February and we left a little hell in May. Even Armentières was not what it was in the days of June 1915.

However it taught us more than ever about trench warfare. It seemed a pity to leave the trenches, concrete tunnels and dug-outs that we had built, but that is always the way.

On our arrival at Rabot, Johnnie [Dashwood] left for the Motor Machine-Gun Corps.[1]

In June 1916 the officers were:–

Commanding Officer	Lt-Col W. J. B. Tweedie
Second-in-command	Major J. C. Scott, DSO
Adjutant	Captain W. S. Stevenson
OC 'A' Company	Captain H. G. Sotheby, MVO
OC 'B' Company	Captain N. A. C. Weir
OC 'C' Company	Captain N. McQueen
OC 'D' Company	Captain C. C. G. Johnstone
OC Machine Guns	Lieut R. W. Davidson
OC Bombs	Lieut E. G. Leggett
OC Transport	Captain F. J. D. Knowling
OC Snipers	Lieut J. S. Stott, DCM
OC Signallers	Lieut D. G. Miller
Quartermaster	Lieut W. R. Weller
Medical Officer	Lieut Nankivell

---

1. Later the Royal Tank Corps.

'B' Company Officers were:– Self, Lieutenant H. McLardy, 2nd Lieutenant C. H. Dickerson, 2nd Lieutenant J. Kennedy, 2nd Lieutenant D. M. Ramsay. Company Sergeant-Major Gilchrist & Company Quartermaster-Sergeant Brodie.

6.

Rest and Training for the 'Big Push'

—————

Weir's 9th Division had been pulled out of the Plug Street sector to prepare for the costliest British attack of the war: the Battle of the Somme. The die had been cast at the Chantilly Conference in early December 1915 when the four Great Powers at war with Germany and Austria-Hungary – Britain, France, Russia and Italy – agreed to launch simultaneous offensives on the Western, Eastern and Italian fronts. It was a personal victory for the French Commander-in-Chief, Marshal Joffre, who had dismissed the failed Gallipoli campaign of 1915 as a sideshow diverting resources from the main effort on the continent.

Later that month Joffre had a private meeting with Sir Douglas Haig, the new commander of the BEF, to discuss the offensive. Haig preferred an attack in Flanders that would strike at the main railway junctions beyond the front line and prevent a German strategic withdrawal (which was easier to carry out from the Somme to the Meuse). But with the instructions of Lord Kitchener ringing in his ears – that the 'closest co-operation between the French and the British as a united Army must be the governing policy' (albeit with the caveat that his command 'is an independent one, and that you will in no case come under the orders of any Allied General further than the necessary co-operation')[1] – he was forced to yield to Joffre's demand that the attack be a joint effort at the point where the British and French lines joined: along the Somme River. The offensive was tentatively set for August when a further 19 of Kitchener's New Army divisions would be available. This would enable 25 British divisions to attack north of the Somme and a further 40 French divisions to the south.

This all changed with the German attack at Verdun in February 1916. The battle raged for the rest of the year (though the worst of the fighting was over by June), by which time the Germans had made little headway at a cost of 355,000 casualties; the French, mostly defending, lost 410,000. The combined

—————

1. Sheffield, *The Chief*, p. 160.

dead were 250,000. But Verdun was just as catastrophic for the BEF because it caused Joffre to appeal for Haig to bring forward the joint offensive to June, and for the British to play the dominant role with 13 divisions advancing on a front of 17 miles, while 11 French divisions moved forward over 8 miles

In a letter dated 5 June, Weir comments on the news that 'the Navy have caught it in the neck this time' and that it is 'no good being so cocksure'. He is referring to the only major sea engagement of the war, the Battle of Jutland, fought between the Royal Navy's Grand Fleet and the German Imperial Navy's High Seas Fleet off the Jutland peninsula on 31 May 1916. The fleets were comprised of 28 Dreadnoughts, 9 battlecruisers, 8 armoured cruisers, 26 light cruisers, 78 destroyers, a seaplane-carrier and a minesweeper on the British side, and 16 Dreadnoughts, 6 pre-Dreadnoughts, 5 battlecruisers, 11 light cruisers and 61 destroyers on the German.

After a battlecruiser action, the two main fleets clashed twice. The British sustained heavier losses – 3 battlecruisers, 4 armoured cruisers and 8 destroyers (6,094 sailors) to 1 battlecruiser, 1 pre-Dreadnought, 4 light cruisers and 5 destroyers (2,551 sailors) – before the German fleet slipped away in the dark, having earlier broken off the engagement because of the heavier British fire. It was because of the disparity of losses that some observers, Weir included, saw Jutland as a tactical defeat. Yet the outcome was undoubtedly a strategic victory for Britain, confirming its naval superiority; never again would the German High Seas Fleet leave port during the war.[1]

As preparation for the Battle of the Somme, Weir notes that he and his men had to undergo 'special open warfare and offensive training'. They were following guidelines laid down by *SS109 Training of Divisions for Offensive Action*, a recently issued pamphlet that contained basic tactical advice for the coming battle. The pamphlet stipulated the marking out of 'a complete system of hostile trenches' from trench maps and aerial photographs, whereupon the whole division should practise assaulting it 'several times'.

It added:

> Every attacking unit must be given a limited and clearly defined objective, which it is to capture and consolidate at all costs; the assaulting columns must go right through above ground to this objective in successive waves or lines, each line adding fresh impetus to the preceding line when this is checked, and carrying the whole forward to the objective.

The concluding paragraph read:

> It must be impressed on all ranks that a 'decisive success in battle can be gained only by a vigorous offensive', and in no operation of war is

---

1. Statistics for the Battle of Jutland from Keegan, *The First World War*, pp. 294–6.

rapidity and determination more important than in exploiting a success after breaking through a hostile system of defences.[1]

War Diary June 1916

We were now due for a long 'rest', but that doesn't mean rest in the sense of peace and quiet, it means rest from the guns. Thus as will be seen later we had now to undergo special open warfare and offensive training. This training eventually led us to the Somme battlefield, but of course we were unaware at the time as to what sort of work we were wanted for. On leaving Rabot, we marched just beyond Steenwerck and spent a night at Le Verrier, an uncomfortable hamlet. The next day we proceeded through Doulieu (where Jasper Carew was buried), Neuf-Berquin (where we marched past General Plumer, who had come to bid the division a good-bye), La Motte, a pretty little village in the Forêt de Nieppe to Morbecque. Here we billeted the night.

During our day here we were pleased to hear that Colonel Tweedie had got the CMG and Dick Knowling the MC. On again the next day through the town of Aire and Quernes to Enquin-les-Mines, which as its name implies, is a mining village. Here we had quite a comfortable billet miles away from the guns. The Divisional Headquarters were at Bomy.

Just at this time Knowling left us to take the job of acting Staff Captain to the 27th Brigade, so Kenneth Thomson took the Transport. Major Scott also left and his place as second-in-command was taken by Sotheby. Captain McFarlane was placed in command of 'A' Company. 2nd Lieutenant Colin Mitchell joined 'B' Company.

To Mrs Edith Weir

Enquin-les-Mines
[Monday] 5 June 1916

My Dear Mother,

I am very sorry I haven't written lately but we have had such a lot of moving about. I now have a billet in a girls' school – some billet! I expect you have seen the Birthday Honours. Knowling has got the MC – lucky devil – he has done very good work.

I only wish these things would come my way – no such luck. He has also managed to get a staff job, so that leaves me alone of all those who came out with the Regiment. I must start pulling the strings. The weather is just so grand now.

---

1. *SS109 Training of Divisions for Offensive Action*, Imperial War Museum SS/CDS Pamphlet Collection.

I got a parcel from Auntie Bea and the D[illegible] as well. When you next write, please thank Auntie Bea from me. I really haven't time to write as I am very shorthanded and such a lot wants setting up. Well the Navy have caught it in the neck this time. It is no good being so cocksure.

I must end now, I hope D. is well.

>   *Yours,*
>   *Neil*

War Diary   June 1916

We spent about three weeks [at Enquin-les-Mines] practising open warfare and tactical training first by companies, then by battalions and brigades. Our next move was to entrain at Berguette Station for the Amiens Area. After a long journey we detrained at a small station just outside this town called [illegible] and marched right through the town to the village of St-Sauveur. Here again we had comfortable billets. Now at last we were in the 4th Army (General Rawlinson) and so might expect something to happen.

This time our training was more progressive and the officers and men took a greater interest because we knew perfectly well that we were in for another big show.

There were constant proofs of this. The massing of big guns, more aircraft observation, a large concentration of cavalry and infantry. During our time here certain officers (myself included) went up in buses to Bray, a town quite near the front line. From there we walked up to the trenches opposite Montauban, which were then held by the 30th Division of the 13th Corps (General Congreve).

The trenches were quite different to any we had seen before. White chalk predominated everywhere and the country round was as flat as a pancake. The masses of guns, chiefly French 75 mms, proved to us that this really was to be a push. We were given to understand that the 9th Division would be the reserve division to the 13th Corps. The other divisions in the Corps were the 18th & 30th Divisions. These were to be the assaulting divisions. We were to follow up.

On our return from an eventful day we stopped in Corbie, the Divisional Headquarters, and then had a good dinner in the pub there. We then carried on our training a few days longer during which time Thomson (who had returned) again went off to the Machine-Gun Corps and McLardy went sick with pleurisy. 2nd Lieutenant Andrews joined the Company.

To **Mrs Edith Weir**   *Somme Sector*
                                                    [Tuesday] 20 June 1916

My Dear Mother,

Just a line to say I am quite well – hoping you are the same. All our regiments sent their pipes and drums last night and had a combined band which caused much excitement amongst the villagers. I think our Band is quite the best. Owing to a tremendous amount of work my letters are not so regular. You mustn't expect me to write every day, as I don't seem to have a moment to myself. Uncle Hugh has joined the RAMC, I hear. Do you ever see Harry Hill now? There are a great many ditches and jumps where we are and I get my nag to practise jumping. I have not had a spill yet, but I expect one daily.

Cheeroh.

                    With love,
                    Neil

War Diary   June 1916

26 June 1916: We then entrained again and spent a night in Corbie and two nights at a place called Vaux on the Somme under canvas. Here my horse pitched me into a bog.

All this time we were preparing for the offensive by getting together bombs, small arms ammunition etc. and each company was given a distinguishing colour. 'A' Company were red, 'B' Company were yellow, 'C' Company were blue and 'D' Company were green. Everyone now was in fighting order and our valises were stacked at Corbie.

Divisional Headquarters now shifted up to its battle position at Grove Town and so we will break off here and come to the First Battle of the Somme.

7.

The Battle of the Somme

At 7:30 a.m. on 1 July 1916, after a week-long bombardment in which a million shells were fired, fourteen British divisions and six French moved forward into no-man's land on either side of the Somme river. Sir Douglas Haig had anticipated a battle that would unfold in stages, possibly over a prolonged period. In that sense it was for Haig a 'step by step' attack with each 'bound forward by the Infantry' dependent 'on the area which has been prepared by the Artillery'.[1] A day earlier his Intelligence chief, Brigadier-General Charteris, had written:

> We do not expect any great advance, or any great place of arms to fall. We are fighting primarily to wear down the German armies and the German nation, to interfere with their plans, gain some valuable position and generally to prepare for the great decisive offensive which must come sooner or later.[2]

If, however, the attack broke through the first two German lines on 1 July, the cavalry would be committed in a more ambitious role. As Haig's biographer Gary Sheffield put it: 'Hoping for a major triumph, perhaps he expected something less dramatic, planning for various degrees of success.'[3]

But even Haig's more limited aims were to be disappointed on 1 July. North of the old Roman road (Albert–Bapaume) that bisected the battlefield there was almost complete failure to take even the first of the three German defensive lines. The only significant gains were to the south where two British Corps, the XV and XIII (whose reserve formation was Weir's 9th Division), and the French Sixth Army captured most of their objectives. The 'butcher's bill' for the BEF's sketchy performance, meanwhile, was 57,470 men, of whom 19,240 were killed or died of wounds, the bloodiest day in the British Army's history.[4]

---

1. Quoted in Sheffield, *The Chief,* p. 165.
2. Ibid., p. 164.
3. Ibid., p. 166.
4. Statistics quoted in ibid., p. 170.

There were further minor attacks on 2 July and the days thereafter (costing a further 25,000 casualties), but the next major push was not until 14 July when the Fourth Army used the two corps that had won the biggest gains on the first day of the battle, the XV and XIII, to attack the German Second Position between Longueval and Bazentin-le-Petit. The bombardment of this second position by 1,000 guns began on 11 July with eighteen times the weight of shell per yard of trench to be attacked than had been used on the 1st. 'The whole horizon', noted an observer, 'seemed to be bursting shells in front of us, and behind us flashing guns.'[1]

Four divisions were assigned to the assault: the 21st and 7th of XV Corps on the left, and the 3rd and 9th of XIII Corps on the right, with the 18th Division supporting the attack by clearing Trônes Wood. The task of Weir's brigade, the 26th, was to take Waterlot Farm and the lower part of the village of Longueval, while its sister brigades, the 27th and South African, took upper Longueval and Delville Wood respectively.

To gain surprise, the assaulting troops were moved forward at night into no-man's land where white tapes had been laid to mark the jumping-off point. Most histories attribute the job of laying out the tapes to parties of Royal Engineers, but Weir's diary is explicit on this point: the man responsible was the battalion adjutant, Captain W. E. Stevenson (known to Weir and his friends as 'Staggers'). Weir also confirms that, while some casualties were sustained by random shelling, the Germans never discovered their intention.

The attack began at dawn, after a brief five-minute 'hurricane' bombardment, with the assaulting troops protected by a 'creeping' barrage that lifted fifty yards every one and a half minutes to give the Germans no time to re-man their machine-guns before the enemy was upon them. By mid-morning more than 6,000 yards of the German Second Position – including the villages of Bazentin-le-Petit, Bazentin-le-Grand and part of Longueval and Delville Wood – were in British hands. In the neighbouring XV Corps' sector, meanwhile, an opportunity to make a decisive breakthrough that day was lost because it took too long to bring the cavalry supports forward; while on XIII Corps' front a series of determined counter-attacks by a fresh German division, the 7th, prevented Weir's 9th Division from completing the capture of either Longueval or Delville Wood. The 10th Argylls, however, had achieved all of their objectives, and Weir's diary gives a graphic description of his part in this successful action. Haig, for his part, described 14 July as the 'best day we have had this war',[2] no small endorsement in the context of almost two years of combat.

Later that month the attacks on the Somme continued with Imperial troops (Australians and South Africans) taking Pozières and Delville Wood, but no

---

1. Philpott, *Bloody Victory*, p. 238.
2. Quoted in Sheffield, *The Chief*, p. 183.

opportunity for the cavalry to intervene recurred. By 31 July, the Germans had lost 160,000 men; the British and French more than 200,000, yet the line had moved barely three miles since 1 July. North of the Ancre, or along half the original front, it had scarcely moved at all.[1]

War Diary   Summer 1916

28 June: After leaving Vaux we marched up to the Bois des Celestines, a woody eminence overlooking the River Somme. Here we went into huts and stayed three days. The battle had commenced [on 1 July] and we were constantly receiving news of its progress, as there was an aeroplane landing station quite close to our huts. We did nothing much at Celestine but Dickerson amused us very much in his attempts to get champagne or rather the local fizz.

I should at this point perhaps mention that we were the reserve brigade of the division and the South African Brigade and 27th Brigade were ahead of us the whole time.

Our next stage was a move to Grove Town, where we slept in the open. No doubt this brought on a lot of pleurisy which soon followed as the nights were exceedingly cold. As a matter of fact CSM Gilchrist had to go to hospital but luckily he returned two or three days later.

Then we went further up to dug-outs in Billon Wood (Billon Wood was a great place for guns; our pipers danced to amuse the French), while the 27th Brigade had already entered the fight and taken Bernafay Wood so we shifted up to the open at Carnoy just behind the original front line.

From here we went up to explore the newly won positions between Montauban and Bernafay Wood. The 27th Brigade, who were holding the trenches in the latter place, were having very heavy casualties so it was necessary to relieve them by the 26th Brigade.

My Company was given a bit of a trench to hold between the Wood and Montauban itself. In front of this trench there was a quarry which the Boche had transformed into headquarters dug-outs.

Thus 'B' Company's hard time started before we were actually wanted for an advance.

This was a trench in name only, in fact an old Boche communication trench. Naturally we were shelled continually and the consequence was I had about twenty casualties which considerably weakened my platoons. CSM Gilchrist received a nasty bit of shell in the shoulder which caused him considerable trouble afterwards. Sergeant Logan took on the duties of Company Sergeant-Major.

---

1. Keegan, *The First World War*, p. 319.

In addition to the shelling it rained like hell so things were very bad and depressing. Luckily the Boche had had the wind taken out of him for the time being and he was nearly 1,000 yards off.

After three days of this 'B' & 'D' Companies were sent back to Carnoy for one night. 'D' Company had been holding Montauban itself and on relief were heavily shelled, losing a brave officer called Drummond. At this point Captain C. C. G. Johnstone went sick and Lieutenant R. I. Smith took over 'D' Company. Glass of 'D' Company was also wounded so they suffered badly in officers.

The next night [in fact morning, as the attack went in at dawn], July 14th, we went up again to our previous position and out into no-man's land to take up our station for an assault on Longueval.

This attack was part of the second stage of the battle. On our right we had the 8th Black Watch supported by the 7th Seaforths and we were the left battalion of the 26th Brigade and surrounded by the 5th Camerons. The 12th Royal Scots of the 27th Brigade were drawn up on the left of the Battalion. The objective of the 9th Division was to seize Waterlot Farm, Delville Wood and the village of Longueval.

The South Africans were to take Delville Wood, the 26th Brigade to take Waterlot Farm and near half of the village, while the 27th Brigade were to make a right wheel and seize the upper part of the village. Unfortunately Trônes Wood on the Division's right flank had not been taken in the 1st stage, although the 30th Division had made several gallant attempts to do so.

The Battalion dispositions were as follows:

'B' Company supported by 'D' Company on the right with a platoon frontage and depth of four lines per company.

'A' Company supported by 'C' Company on the left in touch with the 12th Royal Scots.

We were in touch with the 8th Black Watch on the right.

The Company's objective was to capture and consolidate the line from the crossroads in the village to a point called Piccadilly about 200 yards to the left. The name of this line was Clarges Street. 'A' Company was to continue Clarges Street to the left, while 'D' & 'C' Companies were to consolidate the support line called Dover Street.

My platoons were drawn up as follows:

1st Wave	No. 5 Platoon under Platoon Sergeant Lyle
2nd Wave	No. 8 Platoon under 2nd Lieutenant Colin Mitchell
3rd Wave	No. 7 Platoon under 2nd Lieutenant Ramsay
	Company Headquarters

4th Wave   No. 6 Platoon under Lieutenant Dickerson
                   This was the carrying platoon

Our right-hand man rested on the road leading to Bernafay Wood. The entry into no-man's land to take up our positions until the dawn was a tricky business. It was the first time that the British Army had attempted an assault from such a position.

However our positions were well taped out [marked with white tape] by Stevenson, the Adjutant, and we had no difficulty in finding them quietly.

Unfortunately the Boche was shelling no-man's land hard and naturally we had some casualties. I thought that the men's groans would give our positions away, but the Boche didn't seem to suspect anything.

The only people that troubled us were the snipers in Trônes Wood on our right flank.

Thus we lay and waited for dawn when our hurricane bombardment was to commence. It was a dreadful and damp wait but as the dawn came so our guns started until they reached a tremendous intensity and at a real outburst from the 18-pounders just behind us, we knew that it was time for us to go forward and, raising ourselves from our cramped positions, we moved first at a walk and then broke into a double over the 400 yards that separated us from our friend the Boche.

During the advance, which commenced at a walking pace breaking gently into a double, we could see little for smoke caused by the explosion of our shells and mortars. The noise too was terrific and yet I could distinctly hear the 'tap – tap' of the Boche machine guns away to our right.

In such circumstances men get out of all control and consequently my two front platoons dashed on towards their objective, meeting with little opposition. Unfortunately we were too quick for the gunners who had not lifted, and so these keen men dashed into their own barrage. This did not help matters so we came back fifty yards or so and got back into some kind of formation.

We then advanced once more and reached the crossroads at Longueval at the same time as the Black Watch on our right. And this is where the officers come in, i.e. to re-organise and get the men to consolidate. Which we did.

The Black Watch and some Seaforths hauled some fifty-odd Boche prisoners out of a deep dug-out and setting them out in the square were about to shoot them wholesale. This was done in the excitement of the moment and luckily we were able to stop it. Assuredly they would have shot them. The Boche doubled down towards our back lines – willingly!

No. 5 & No. 6 Platoons then started to dig our strongpoint just to the left of the crossroads and practically touching Clarges Street.

I established my Headquarters and Lewis gunners in a deep dug-out, evidently an old Boche headquarters – a comfortable spot.

No. 7 Platoon was put in company support in an old Boche communication trench off Piccadilly and No. 6 Platoon were put in company reserve in a fairly strong trench between Clarges Street and Dover Street.

It is interesting to know that the attack was timed to start at 3:25 a.m. and we reached our objective at about 4:15 a.m. When my Company got disorganised when moving on the objective I got Wilson, the piper, to play the Regimental March, which he did in grand style, thus reassembling the Company.

It was now about 5:00 a.m. and I moved along attended by my orderly to get in touch with the Company on the right and left and also with Battalion Headquarters.

I soon found Colonel Tweedie who had taken up his Headquarters in a big shell hole in Clarges Street. Stevenson was with him with a slight wound in the finger. The Colonel had nearly been hit with a bomb and was very deaf. I had received a scrape from a machine-gun bullet in the right knee. McFarlane of 'A' Company had a bad one in the wrist and was ordered down the line. Woodruff took over 'A' Company. We also got touch with 'C' Company who were digging a strongpoint just to our left on the other side of Piccadilly. They had relieved 'A' Company who had only one officer left.

I had lost Mitchell, Company Sergeant-Major Logan and Sergeant Lyle wounded, just to mention one or two casualties.

The road called Piccadilly between my Company and 'C' Company was a perfect death trap as the Boche had snipers and a machine gun playing down the road. Consequently all were cautioned not to cross the road. However poor Dickerson, Officer Commanding No. 6 [Platoon], was killed in crossing at the double and we buried him just near our redoubt. The chief excitement in the afternoon was that eight Boches who were concealed in a dug-out just behind our Headquarters broke out and commenced to assail No. 7 Platoon with bombs. They were soon surrounded but put up a sturdy fight, the oldest of the party being nearly mad with rage. They were all killed.

On completion of our redoubt I withdrew No. 5 Platoon alongside No. 8 Platoon in reserve. Battalion Headquarters had moved back to a trench, (the original Boche front line) behind Dover Street and established touch by runner.

Now if all had gone well, the 27th Brigade should have right-wheeled and occupied the north-east of the village in front of us. This they failed to do as the Boche had got back into some strongpoints up there, although my bombers had cleared them out in the morning. The 27th Brigade spent all the day trying to clear and reach their objective but failed to do so. Thus 'B' Company were holding the front line in a very disadvantageous position. The South African Brigade's left flank was in the air in Delville Wood. Nothing happened the rest of the day. In fact the Boche were very quiet. What were they up to? Thus ended July 14th.

15 July: Preparations had been made to get the Boche out of the northern end of the village under cover of darkness. Our battalion bombers unknown to me or my Company went out on our left flank and returned in front of our strongpoint. This caused our men to fire, as very naturally they thought they were the Boche attacking. Perhaps they were but our bombers under Leggett never returned and when [I was] going up to the strongpoint to see what the matter was with my orderly, McFadden, another disaster overtook us. McFadden was shot right through the lung and we had to get him down on an old door as all our stretchers were in use. (McFadden was the hero at Loos.) I also heard that Reid, who had been my servant for some time and had just married, had had his leg blown away.

Andrews came up from the transport during the night and took No. 6 Platoon.

The rest of the night passed quietly but the Boche was still in the village. My signallers made themselves useful and made tea and we drank it out of beautiful china mugs as the house above us had evidently been a china shop at one time or other.

I couldn't rest, nor could anyone else, so I went over to visit the Black Watch company on our right.

The crossroads in the village was another place to avoid as the Boche sniped down there and I lost most of my orderlies taking the written messages across it. We were quite thankful to see the dawn of the 15th day.

One had got some idea by now of the officer casualties we had sustained the previous day. 'A' Company had lost Falconer-Stewart, Cassie and McFarlane, the former [*sic*] died of his wounds. 'B' Company had lost Dickerson killed and Mitchell killed. 'C' Company lost De Burgh, who was badly wounded in the jaw. Headquarters had lost the Medical Officer, Nankivell, badly wounded in the stomach, and Leggett [Bombing Officer] who was killed. RSM Eadie was also killed. Stott, the Sniping Officer, had been wounded.

Nothing really happened on the 15th or 16th. We were certainly very heavily shelled but the Boche had received a hard knock and he was still well employed in Delville Wood, which the South Africans were consolidating step by step. The 27th Brigade also made spasmodic attempts to capture the rest of the village without success. Brigadier-General Tudor, the Commander Royal Artillery, visited me and elicited much information about the artillery barrage.

The morning of the 17th opened well for us. The 76th Brigade, which included the 1st Gordons, came through and succeeded in clearing the rest of the village. The capture of the whole of Delville Wood was also reported. The 76th Brigade spent the rest of the day consolidating and then handed over to the 27th Brigade. That night the Boche put a heavy gas shell bombardment on the roads behind the lines as the transport was coming up. Kenneth Thomson, the Transport Officer, was killed as was also old Weller, the Quartermaster. Weller had been with the Battalion since August 1914, Thomson was an original 'B' Company man in Bramshott days. Laidlaw of 'C' Company was hit in the head and never recovered and Murray, the Assistant Adjutant was killed by shell fire when carrying messages. It was also reported that Knowling, who was now acting Staff Captain to the 27th Brigade, had been badly wounded in the hand. Old 'Pippy' Aitken also received a hit and had to go down the line after much persuasion from the Colonel. However, we were well satisfied though tired.

The dawn of the 18th opened with a terrific bombardment from the Boche and it was evident that he intended to attack with fresh troops. This is a day I shall never forget.

At 8:00 a.m. the shelling was intense and everything was knocked sky high. My strongpoint was knocked out of recognition and I ordered Ramsay to get part of his platoon back to the line behind while I kept the machine guns with me.

And we were not the only ones moving. It was quite obvious that the Boche had driven the South Africans out of Delville Wood. Heavy firing broke out to our right and we could see the Black Watch retiring. McQueen however hung on at his point, although the 27th Brigade had melted away. This brought us to about 3 p.m. and this is how the situation appeared to 'B' Company.

None of the messages I sent to Headquarters were answered, but an orderly told me that everyone was withdrawing to Dover Street. Orders were therefore given to the Company to form on the line between Clarges Street and Dover Street. And not before it was time as in a few more minutes we would have been surrounded.

The Boche were on us like a knife as their bombardment ceased. Masses of grey figures were to be seen coming across the then no-man's land. We had left our trench and formed up with the rest on Dover Street. What a collection of men there were there and it was found to be exceedingly difficult to obtain any hold on them. Some had been so knocked about that they wanted to get right back to Billon Wood. That was fatal. Luckily better counsel was forthcoming and we held our strong line at Dover Street and mowed down plenty of grey figures. Their thirteen battalions gradually wavered and melted away and at 5:00 p.m. it was decided to counter-attack with our reinforcements, the 32nd Division.

My small Company of about thirty strong managed to dislodge a Boche machine gun in our old strongpoint and we recaptured our original positions. Sergeant McCulloch, then Officer Commanding No. 6 Platoon, was killed in this attempt. On getting back to my old headquarters I found my signet ring, which had dropped off, and also the pipes I had given to the company. The Boche had no time to appropriate either. We were then relieved by the 6th King's Own Scottish Borderers. We in our turn went over the road and relieved the 8th Black Watch.

Needless to say things were in a chaotic state. We had lost touch with the Brigade but the Division was represented by Major McNamara, who was caught up in the line when the counter-attack started.

'B' and 'C' Companies were both ordered to retake Delville Wood with about thirty men each. 'D' Company, however, were detailed for this wild-cat scheme with disastrous results. R. I. Smith, the Company Commander, and Lieutenant S. R Wilson were both killed, as was also R. S. Allen. They came back without so much as getting to the outskirts of the wood.

The next day [19 July] at about 3:00 p.m. we were relieved by the Bantam Division[1] and were ordered back to Carnoy. We didn't take long to get there. After an attempted wash the remnants marched out next day [20 July] to tents at Méaulte, where we could not hear the guns quite so much.

And remnants they were. I still had my two officers, Ramsay and Andrews, but what a few men. Quartermaster-Sergeant Donnachie was Company Sergeant-Major and Company Quartermaster-Sergeant combined. At Méaulte we received a few officer reinforcements. French came back once more. Captain Anderson took command of 'A' Company and Lieutenant Russell took over 'D'.

To **Mrs Edith Weir**   *Méaulte, Somme Area*
                                          [Thursday[20 July 1916

My Dearest Mother,

At last I get an opportunity to write – what a time I have had. I have had the luck to get through another battle although how I escaped God

---

1. The 35th Division, a New Army formation composed of men under the minimum regulation height of 5 ft. 3 in., but otherwise fit for service.

only knows. We are now back to reorganize. The British Army is doing well and our Battalion has had its share as we managed to take a village. I am still very dirty and I know you will be horrified when I say I have been badly bitten by German fleas. I have not had a wash for ages.

You know my signet – that was lost. However luckily I saw a man wearing it and he thought it was a Boche souvenir. Fighting still continues and in places the Hun resists very stubbornly. Nevertheless this is the beginning of the end. Well I am safe and sound – thank God! Knowling was wounded.

Cheeroh.

Yours,
Neil

P.S. I haven't shaved for over a week, what a beard I have!

To Mrs Edith Weir

Méaulte, Somme Area
[Friday] 21 July 1916

My Dear Mother,

Just a line to say I am quite well. We are having a rest from all the worries of the last few days. You might see me in the casualty roll as slightly wounded – but it was nothing to shout about. I was glad to get your letter last night. I enclose another souvenir found on a Boche.

With love,
Neil

War Diary   July 1916

The next day, July 21st, we left the Somme area. Entraining at Méricourt, we detrained at Condé beyond Amiens and marched out to Vauchelles [-lès-Domart?] where we stayed about two days in good billets. The Battalion Headquarters were in the exceptionally fine château, much to the Brigade's disgust. Back to Condé again and a train northward to Bryas [Bours?]. From here we had an 8-mile march to the town of Bruay. And thus we left the 4th Army and joined the 1st Army once more.

All I can say about the battle of Longueval is that it was a better show than Loos.

8.

Vimy Ridge

———>☙<———

From late July to early September 1916, the 9th Division was stationed near Vimy Ridge in Artois. It was during this period that Weir heard he had been recommended for a Distinguished Service Order by his commanding officer, Colonel Tweedie, for gallantry during the Battle of Longueval. Certainly his bravery on 18 July, when he led a successful counter-attack, would seem to justify Tweedie's recommendation. But it was never confirmed and he had to be content with a much less prestigious Mention in Despatches.

War Diary   July 1916

26 July: On entering Bruay we were now as I have already said back with the First Army (Lieutenant-General R. C. B. Haking, as temporary in command) and the Fourth Corps, Lieutenant-General H. Wilson, afterwards CIGS.

Bruay itself was a prosperous mining town some twenty miles behind the line. Our stay here was quite short, but we had time to brush up and have our photos taken. I have the group now.

The next news was that Colonel Tweedie, who had been far from well since the effects of the bomb at Longueval, was invalided down the line so Major H. G. Sotheby was placed temporarily in command. I was at this time made Pipe and Band President and had the task of getting the Band back to its former strength, as we had lost most of our pipers and drummers. McQueen, Stevenson and I were also specially elated when we heard we had been recommended for the DSO, although the Brigade changed all the recommendations to MCs.

28 July: From Bruay we marched up nearer the line to billets in Estrée Gauché [Estrée-Cauchy?]. The place was a fair size village with a single street. Here we trained and received reinforcements. My new officers were Lieutenant J. Mackie, 2nd Lieutenants Crichton, Douglas, McCallum, McCorquodale and Wilson. The latter only remained with me a short time. Sergeant Nicholson (a great man killed soon after I left) of 'D' Company became the Company Sergeant-Major and Company Sergeant-Major Craig of 'C' Company became RSM. Sergeant Madigan was still Drum-Major and Corporal McKenzie was in charge of the pipers.

I had to get a new batman, so chose Neil, an old 'B' Company man.

Our new Colonel, Lieutenant-Colonel J. Kennedy, DSO, late Adjutant of the 93rd and late OC 7th Seaforth Highlanders, also arrived at this time.

Divisional Headquarters were at Cambl[a]in l'Abbé.

To **Mrs Edith Weir**   *Estrée-Cauchy, near Vimy Ridge*
                                          [Saturday] 29 July 1916

My Dear Mother,

We have shifted again to a wretched village full of stinks and fleas – what a combination! Colonel Tweedie went down to the lines yesterday – he was not at all well and very overstrung. Before he left he told me that he had put my name in for a DSO which I don't think I will possibly be given. All this is of course a dead secret and must not be divulged. They have made me Band President and as our band is in a bad state – this is rather a thankless sort of job. Do you know any good lady who would like to present a bugle to our regiment – we want six altogether. What about all your rich friends!

Cheeroh.

                              With love,
                              Neil

War Diary   August 1916

After ten days [at Estrée-Cauchy] in reserve to a weak division, the 37th Division (commanded by Count Gleichen), we took over the trenches on the Vimy Ridge.

It will be remembered that the Ridge was captured by the French in September 1915, when they fought the fearful battles of Carency and Souchez. Both these villages still bore signs of the ravage. In fact, they were villages in name only, as there wasn't a habitable house among the ruins. All the villages behind the line there were in the same plight: Mont-St-Eloi with its landmark church tower, Villers-au-Bois and Ablain-St-Nazaire are instances.

The trenches, such as they were, [were] a perfect havoc. Between the front line and supports there was a huge valley, the Zouave Valley. There were no communication trenches across this waste so that if one's company was up in the front line one had the impression that the Boche could push us off the top into the valley below, before our supports could possibly come to our assistance.

Here again we came across the wretched craters and the Boche seemed to be top dog underneath the earth. There were no dug-outs in the trenches except the Company Headquarters situated in the open on the slope down to Zouave Valley.

Only one company was up in line at the time, the rest of the Battalion being distributed in two strong points on the other side of the dip and in the support line, merely so many elephant dug-outs placed into the bank of the Arras–Souchez road.

Our 4th company remained behind in billets with the reserve battalion. It was indeed lucky for us that the Boche troops opposite were battle-tired, in fact they belonged to the Saxon divisions. We rarely saw the infantry and I personally don't believe they held their trenches. Their trench mortars were certainly objectionable but our special sentries always gave us warning of their approach. Their artillery pleased itself by putting an occasional barrage into Zouave Valley, making plenty of noise but doing little harm.

'Windy Bill' [General Furse] who was still our divisional general soon got us to work and fresh trenches appeared like mushrooms in the night. Plenty of mortars were brought up with plenty of ammunition. Our guns also got busy and the Boche trenches were subjected to continuous treatment by these means. On one occasion when 'Windy Bill' was going round with me one of our 18-pounders landed a dud at our feet. It was lucky it was a dud!

'B' Company held this front piece on nearly every occasion i.e. five to six times. We were lucky not to get many casualties. Crichton was hit by a piece of mortar, but returned two or three weeks later. Douglas fell sick and Captain [George] Denham joined my Company as second-in-command. Stevenson, who had been Adjutant since Ypres, left as Staff Captain to the South African Brigade and this started him off on his road to the Division[al Staff]. Our times out of the line were spent at [Estrée-Cauchy], Gouy-Servins, Camblain l'Abbé and Villers-au-Bois.

26 August: We also spent a considerable time at Beguin near the Corps Headquarters, where we were practising to make raids on the Boche and also an attack on Vimy Ridge. During this time we were inspected by General Haking and General Wilson. The former, who was shortly afterwards relieved by General Horne,[1] McCorquodale's uncle, said that we were the best turned-out unit in the division.

---

1. Lieutenant-General Sir Henry (later General Lord) Horne (1861–1929). A Royal Artilleryman, Horne distinguished himself in the battles of 1914 (particularly Mons where

The attack practices were really quite successful and we all felt sure that it would be quite an easy matter to take the ridge in conjunction with the Naval (63rd) Division on our left and the 60th (London Territorial) Division on our right.

During our practices we experimented with new smoke bombs and my company succeeded in temporarily blinding General Wilson with one, at which he was very wroth.

Shortly after, when we took over the trenches again, we were suddenly relieved by the 24th Division, whose DAQMG [Deputy Assistant Quartermaster-General] was Glencairn Campbell our 1st Adjutant.

We spent one night at Mingoval, during which time I visited Aubigny and then left the 4th Corps and Vimy area.

This brought us to the beginning of September 1916. There is nothing much more to be said about Vimy, except that the Ridge was eventually captured by the Canadians.

To Mrs Edith Weir

Vimy Ridge Area
[Friday] 1 September 1916

My Dear Mother,

Cheers to you! I hope you and D[orothy] are well. The immediate rewards to officers in the division have come out. No Argyll is mentioned – the Seaforths have carried off all ours – it is rotten. We shall have to wait.

The Army Commander [Haking] inspected us yesterday and the Div[isional] General [Furse] told him I had done well. He was quite a nice man. He told us we have the best battalion. I must say I am feeling rather run down – I want a rest badly. I suppose my affairs are going all right. I never hear from Whatley. You might enquire to see my pass book at the Capital & Counties [Bank] Ltd when you are over in Malvern one day.

Yrs,
Neil

---

he covered the retreat) and was given command of the 2nd Division in December 1914, XV Corps in January 1916, and First Army from September 1916 to the end of the war. He was responsible for the introduction of the 'creeping barrage', used with some success during the Battle of the Somme, and his successes included Vimy Ridge in April 1917 and various actions on the left flank of the BEF during the summer of 1918. In 1897 he married Kate McCorquodale, 2nd Lieutenant McCorquodale's aunt.

From **Military Secretary, War Office** *to* **Mrs Edith Weir** *Telegram*
1 September 1916

The Military Secretary presents his compliments to Mrs Weir and begs to inform her that the following report has just been received. Captain N. A. C. Weir, 10th Batt., Argyll & Sutherland Highlanders, was wounded on July 16th but remained at Duty.

9.

Back to the Somme

Weir's 9th Division returned to the Somme in early September to prepare for a new offensive. Though further attacks in August had made little headway, Haig was now convinced that the enemy had 'exhausted his reserves' and 'the crisis of the battle' was at hand.[1] He put his faith in a new secret weapon known as a 'tank' (a name chosen to deceive the Germans). Forty-nine of these early Mark I tanks were used in the attack at Flers on 15 September (a battle in which the 9th Division did not take part). Their appearance terrified the German defenders and the accompanying infantry were able to cover almost two miles before mechanical breakdowns, ditchings in rough ground and enemy fire halted the advance. The territory gained 'was about twice that gained on 1 July and at about half the cost in casualties';[2] but there was no decisive breakthrough partly because Rawlinson, commanding the Fourth Army, had kept the cavalry too far back to take advantage.

Nevertheless the operation was considered a success and to build on it, and other modest Anglo-French gains on the Somme in September, Haig planned another series of attacks in October towards what was now the fourth German position along the Transloy ridges in front of Bapaume. In one of the first attacks, on 7 October, the 23rd Division captured the village of Le Sars. Two days later, while the 9th Division was preparing to follow up the 23rd's success with an assault on a German stronghold known as the Butte de Warlencourt, Weir was badly wounded in the left thigh by a German flare and evacuated back to Britain. Fortunately his leg was saved by a new way of healing burns known as the Ambrine Wax Treatment. Invented before the war by a French doctor, Barthe de Sandfort, the treatment involved coating the wound with an airtight wax made of resin mixed with paraffin, which dulled the pain, prevented infection and, in some cases, allowed the wound to heal without scarring. Even so, Weir would remain in hospital until December 1916.

Meanwhile Weir's former company had spearheaded the 10th Argylls'

---

1. Quoted in Sheffield, *The Chief*, p. 188.
2. Ibid., p. 190.

attack on the Butte de Warlencourt on 10 October. The assault failed, as would three more that month, and 'B' Company alone lost 40 killed, wounded and missing (the exact list was sent to Weir in hospital), so many, in fact, that by early November the company was being commanded by a 2nd lieutenant. Heavy rain had long since turned the Somme into a quagmire and, though the attacks continued into November, no more significant gains were made.

When the Allied offensive was officially brought to a halt on 19 November, the furthest line of advance was at Les Boeufs, seven miles forward of the German line on 1 July. The British alone had suffered 419,000 casualties (including Raymond Asquith, son of the Prime Minister, killed near Flers on 15 September); the French 194,451; and the Germans as many as 600,000 (though the figures have never been verified).[1] In his dispatch on the battle, entitled 'The Opening of the Wearing-Out Battle', Haig implied that he had never sought a decisive engagement (which was not true, though he had always accepted the possibility of settling for attrition). Instead he argued that the 'main objects' of the battle had been attained: 'Verdun had been relieved; the main German forces had been held on the Western front; and the enemy's strength had been very considerably worn down'.[2]

War Diary   September 1916

After leaving Mingoval, we passed through Tincques and Penin and marched to good billets at Berlencourt. The Battalion occupied the whole of the village. Our fortnight here was spent in fattening up for another bout in the Somme but we didn't know our ultimate destination. The officers were taken out on tactical tours and the men indulged in open warfare tactics. Sports were also much in demand and our new Army Corps Commander, General Fergusson, again came down and presented medals to the Division General. Fergusson was now commanding the 17th Corps. Our Battalion received two DCMs and four MMs.

Anderson took over the transport and [Captain George] Denham took command of 'A' Company. McCorquodale left to go as ADC to his uncle [General Horne, GOC First Army]. Crichton, who had returned, met with a serious bombing accident when our Bombing Officer, Craig, was killed. The officers in 'B' Company were now: Andrews (No. 5 [Platoon]) McCallum (No. 6), Ramsay (No. 7) and Mackie (No. 8)

6 October: Our next step was to billets at a village called Frohen-le-Grand behind Doullens and a good march. We only spent one night here and were then taken in fleets of French motor buses through Doullens, Talmas

1. Keegan, *The First World War*, p. 321.
2. Quoted in Sheffield, *The Chief*, p. 194.

Neil Weir wearing Scottish dress at a young age.

Neil with his mother, Edith Rosa Weir, and his sister, Dorothy Campbell Weir.

Neil in his Keble College, Oxford, blazer.

Neil's War Office portrait.

10th (SERVICE) BATT. ARGYLL & SUTHERLAND HIGHLANDERS.

BRAMSHOTT, 1915.

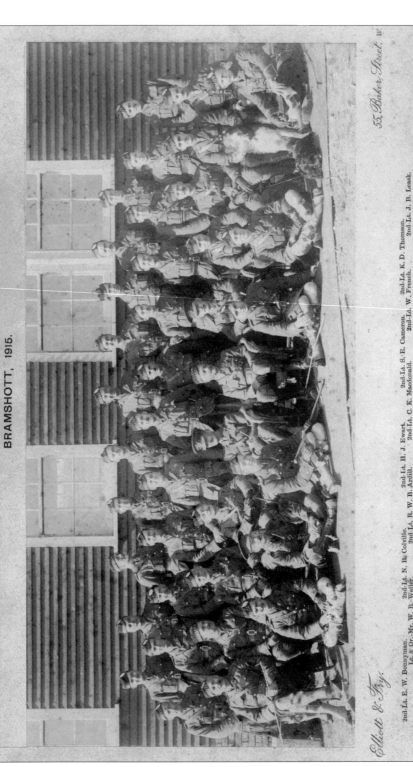

Elliott & Fry.

55, Baker Street. W.

2nd.-Lt. E. W. Bonnyman.   2nd.-Lt. N. R. Colville.   2nd.-Lt. H. J. Ewart.   2nd.-Lt. S. E. Cameron.   2nd.-Lt. K. D. Thomson.
Lt. & Qr.-Mr. W. R. Weller.   2nd.-Lt. R. W. B. Ardill.   2nd.-Lt. C. K. Macdonald.   2nd.-Lt. W. French.   2nd.-Lt. J. B. Leask.
Lt. N. S. Linton.   Capt. W. V. Lumsden.   Lt. F. J. Christison.   Lt. C. L. D. Tully.   2nd.-Lt. F. J. D. Knowling.   2nd.-Lt. J. L. Laidlaw.
Lt. J. H. Beith.   2nd.-Lt. R. S. Fitchie.   2nd.-Lt. C. B. Brownlie.   Lt. J. E. Macmillan.   Lt. N. McQueen.   2nd.-Lt. A. O. T. Deas.
Capt. C. J. Warchope.   Maj. G. W. Muir.   Maj. W. J. B. Tweedie.   Maj. A. I. R. Glasfurd (Brigade Maj.)   Capt. G. D. Campbell.   Capt. A. G. Wade.
Capt. R. N. Macpherson.   Lt.-Col. A. F. Mackenzie, M.V.O.   Maj. R. J. P. Cox.   Capt. & Adj. W. G. Campbell.
Capt. A. H. Walker.   Lt. R. St. A. Heathcote, R.A.M.C.   Lt. R. V. C. Cavendish.   2nd.-Lt. W. S. Stevenson.   2nd.-Lt. Sir J. L. Dashwood.   2nd.-Lt. N. A. C. Weir.
Absent :—Lt. Lord G. Dundas.   Lt. M. D. Graham.   2nd.-Lt. H. M. de Burgh.

N. A. C. Weir photo album, 1914. A selection of images from the pages illustrating his training at Itchen Stoke near Winchester. Miss Skrine and the Rev. Vivan Skrine (*above left*); the rectory (*above right*); a training trench (*below*); the mill (*bottom*).

Left: 2nd Lieutenant Neil Weir (*far right, seated*) with his fellow officers of the 10th Argylls, Bramshott Camp, 1915.

Within the photographs (handwritten captions):

B Company Officers. Cameron, Bonnyman, Self, Major Cox, Laidlaw and Leask.

A Company Officers. Ardish, Capt Walker, Major Muir Cavendish Ewart.

Machine Gun Officers. Christison, Beith, Dashwood.

"Off for a march" R.S.M. Bunnett.

Top left: 'A' Company officers –
Ardish [Ardill?], Capt Walker,
Major Muir, Cavendish, Ewart.

Top right: 'B' Company officers –
Cameron, Bonnyman, Weir,
Major Cox, Laidlaw and Leask.

Above: Machine-gun officers –
Christison, Beith and Dashwood.

Right: 'Off for a march'.
RSM Bunnett marches in front.

C Company Officers.
Pitchie, Knowling, Maj. McPherson, McMillan, McDonald.

Brigade Major, Brigadier, Staff Captain

Some of B Company's Sgts.

Some of No 8 Platoon.

Both pages: The 10th Argylls at Bramshott Camp, March 1915, with Weir's original hand-written captions.

Top left: 'C' Company officers – Pitchie (?), Knowling, Major McPherson, McMillan, McDonald.

Top right: Brigade Major [Major Glasfurd], Brigadier [Brigadier-General Bruce], Staff Captain.

Above: 'B' Company sergeants.

Right: Members of No. 8 Platoon.

French postcards that were included with some of Weir's letters. Some place names have been censored.

Delville Wood, a photograph illustrating the terrain endured by the soldiers in 1916.

'The Pipers at Longueval.' A contemporary artist's view of how the Highlanders
were led into battle on 14 July 1916.

Highlanders from 26th Brigade returning from the trenches after the attack on Longueval.

Longueval after the battle, autumn 1916.

Somerville Hospital
Oxford.

17.10.1916

My Dear Mother,
Just a line to say I have arrived quite happily. This hospital is at Somerville College (the (late) Ladies College — just behind Keble. One of the nurses — a Miss Owen knows all

our part of the country pretty well. The other stays at Temple Langhorne with the Brits. She used to live in Grimley and is Harry Childers' niece. Well you might easily train down one day and see me. I am

Weir's letter from the Somerville College Hospital, Oxford, to his mother, 17 October 1916.

very glad I got here.
Yrs with love
Neil

In the Field
7=11-1916

Dear Sir

I am sending B. Coy Casualties with Mr Ramsay to post on arrival in England as it would probably get censored if sent otherwise. Hope you are speedily moving from your injuries. and able to be about. by this time. We are having a sort of rest just now near the line digging every day but not doing trench duty in the vicinity of "Arras" at a village called "Simencourt." Mr Hackie was left in charge of the Coy when you came a cropper but took sick and has been in Hospl. since. We have a 2d Lt i/c of the Coy now. and are struggling to get the usual deficiencies made

up. We got a draft of 52 to the Coy before they left McSars & Batt de———— warm worn out trenches. they came from the 2/9th. We are settled down and have got the mud scrubbed off and enjoying the hardest rest we have had yet. Mr Andrews & Sgt Hackbacks are on leave just now and Mr Ramsays going today. I suppose you will know all the officers casualties in the Batt from the Papers so am sending the Coy.s only. We are expecting to move back a bit very shortly but probably it is one of the many rumours. Still it looks probable seeing the leave has started. Drop a P.C. if you receive this all right. Cant think on anything else

you would care to know. I hear Sgt Henderson Ptes Sandilands & Robertson (Coy L.G) are being recommended for the Military Medal not a bad pick I believe. All wish you to have a speedy recovery according to what I hear as well as Myself.
                    Yours very
                       Sincerely
                          J.B.

Killed or died of wounds
2nd Lt Wilson
Pte Rutherford. S.B.
  " Balbirnie (8)
  " Atcheson (8) S.B.
  " McConachie (9)
Lcorp Wyatt
Pte McNeill (trench mortar)

Wounded
        Capt Weir
        2nd Lt McCallum.
        L/Sgt Sherman
        Pte Finlayson
7921. " Ross
     " Ritchie
     " Shannon
     " Acton
     " Brady
     " Fleming
     " McGovern

Wounded
        Pte McIntosh (Bomber)
         " McSherry. S.B.
         " Travers
         " Abernethy
         " Coutts
8380.   " Innes
         " McIlvchey.
         " Inglim
         " Leskie
         " Dryden
11848.   " Cockerly
        L/Sgt Wardrop (L.G)
        Pte Howie
14813.   " Wilson
         " Thomson
        Lcpt Thomson (L.G)

Missing
    Sergt Sutherland } Believed wounded
    Pte McFarlane   } am afraid he
     " Waddell   } has gone down
     " Farquharson
     " McDonald   over
     " Clark.

also a good many went to hospl from exposure as it was terrible bad weather. The Batt was the worst I have seen it up to the neck in mud.

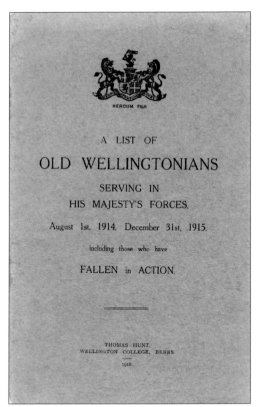

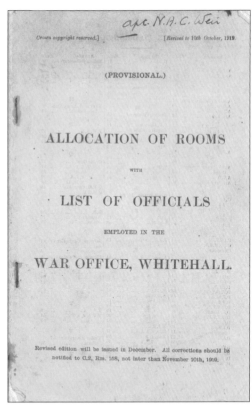

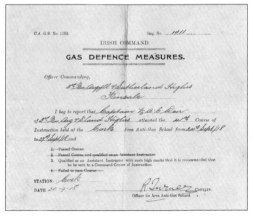

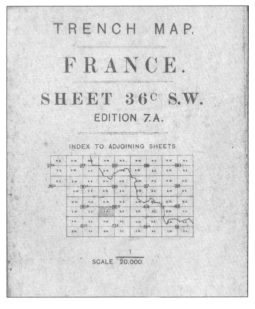

This page: A cross-section of documents preserved by Neil Weir, dating from 1914 to 1920. These include (*below right*), an extract from his confidential report: 'A capable officer of good ability.'

Left: Letter from 'J. B.' (unidentified), written from the Somme on 7 November 1916, to Weir telling him of 'B' Company's casualties since Weir was wounded.

By Direction of Mrs. Weir.

THE COTTAGE

LOWER BROADHEATH, Nr. WORCESTER.

THE REMAINING

FURNITURE

AND EFFECTS

Comprising Butterfly and Egg Cabinets, Mahogany and Walnut Bedroom Suites, Grained and other Wardrobes, Oak and Windsor Arm and other Chairs, Bedsteads,

ANTIQUE OAK CHEST

Walnut Davenport, Copper and Brass Fenders, Toilet Ware, Kitchen Utensils, Magic Lantern and Slides, Phonograph, Musical Box, ¼-plate Camera, Bullseye Kodak, Lady's Saddle, Harness, Wire Netting, Chicken and Duck Rearers, and Houses, Hearson's Patent Foster Mother, 5-barred Iron Hurdles, Cast Iron Tanks and Bins, Chaff Cutter, Lawn Mowers, Ladders, and Miscellaneous Items

WILL BE SOLD BY AUCTION, BY MESSRS.

DEACON & INGMAN

ON THE PREMISES,

ON FRIDAY, OCTOBER 8TH, 1920

AT 11 A.M. ON VIEW MORNING OF SALE.

CATALOGUE.

Auctioneers' Offices: 47, Foregate Street, Worcester (Telephone 513 Worcester), and 3, The Parade, Minehead.

Above: Advert from 1920 for the sale of the contents of 'The Cottage' at Broadheath, Worcestershire. Neil, his mother and his sister moved 50 miles south to Wotton-Under-Edge, Gloucestershire.

Left: Views of their new home, Bourne Stream, Wotton-Under-Edge, Gloucestershire, in 1920. Dorothy Weir is seen at the front gate with her dog Hector.

Neil Weir's family life. His marriage to Hermine Fyffe on 21 August 1930; scenes from their courtship; and with their children; Christina Fyffe Weir, born 18 February 1934, and Celia Campbell Weir, born 8 March 1937.

2nd Lieutenant N. A. C. Weir in 1914, aged 19.

Captain N. A. C. Weir in 1918, aged 23.

Neil Weir in later life, with his wife and daughters. *From left:* Celia Campbell Weir (Mike Burns's mother), Captain Weir, Mrs Hermine Anna Fyffe Weir, Christina Fyffe Weir.

Neil Weir's record of his military service (*left*) and his application to join the Reserve Forces in Nigeria in 1930, during his colonial career (*right*).

No. M.P.24/1928/101.

Divisional Office,
Ogoja, 28th June, 1930.

The Officer Commanding,
3rd Battalion, Nigerian Regiment,
C a l a b a r.

Sir,

European Reserve Force - Application
for appointment

I have the honour to apply for the form of enrolment in the European Reserve, Nigeria (Form N.R.R.1) which I should be obliged if you would send to my home address :-

Bourne Stream,
Holford,
Bridgewater,
Somerset.

as I am proceeding on leave.

2. I am an Administrative Officer aged 35.

My previous military service was from 1914 - 1922 consisting of :-

a. August, 1914 - October, 1916 with the 10th Battalion Argyll and Sutherland Highlanders.

b. October, 1916 - January, 1917 in Hospital (wounded October, 1916).

c. January, 1917 - April, 1918 as instructor and company commander in No. 2, Officer Cadet Battalion.

d. May, 1918 - January, 1919 with the 3rd Battalion Argyll and Sutherland Highlanders including a period on a staff learner's course and an attachment to Headquarters, No.4 Sub District, Cork.

e. January, 1919 - March 1920 attached to the general staff, Military Operations Department, War Office. (demobilised March, 1920)

f. June, 1920 - August, 1922 with the 5th Battalion Gloucestershire Regiment.

3. I am now a Captain on the Territorial Army Reserve of Officers, General list.

I have the honour to be
Sir
Your Obedient Servant,
[signature]
Assistant District Officer.

33

Full Name. NEIL ARCHIBALD CAMPBELL WEIR

Born 25th April 1895.

Present Rank. Captain, E.R.F and T.A. (R of O).

Particulars of Previous Service.

June 1913 to 25th August 1914. Private, Oxford University O.T.C.
26th August 1914. Second Lieutenant (temporary)
7th May 1915 Lieutenant (temporary)
26th September 1915 Captain (temporary).
1st March 1920. Demobilised. Untitled.
24th June 1920. Captain, Territorial Army.
25th August 1922 to present date. Captain, T.A.R. of O.
28th June 1930 to present date. Captain, E.R.F Nigeria.

26. 8. 14 to 19. 9. 14 Officers Training Camp, Churn.
20.9. 14 to 10. 5. 15 10th Bn. Argyll and Sutherland Highlanders (at home).
11. 5. 15 to 15. 10. 16 10th Bn. Argyll and Sutherland Highlanders (B.E.F., France).
Wounded twice. 15. 7. 1916 10.10. 1916.
Mentioned in despatches 1. 1. 1917.
16.10. 16 to 6. 2. 17 Hospital and sick leave.
7. 2. 17 to 28. 4. 18 Instructor and Company Commander No 21 Officer Cadet Battalion (graded as a staff captain while company commander) from 10.1.1917.
29. 4. 18 to 14. 1. 19 3rd Bn. Argyll and Sutherland Highlanders (in Ireland).
Including a Staff Learners Course with 69th Division, Retford, and period of attachment to No.4 Sub-District, Cork.
15. 1. 19 to 1. 3. 20. Attached General Staff, Military Operations Department, War Office.

and Contay (5th Army Headquarters) to Franvillers. Here we spent one night and then marched to Albert, which was now some miles behind the front. Albert we have all heard of. It is famous for the statuette of the Virgin, which was then hanging from the battered clock tower of the cathedral. The town was desolation itself and there were so many troops in the town that it was difficult to find billets and there was an awful muddle up. We were now in the 3rd Corps (Lieutenant-General W. P. Pulteney). Our Divisional Headquarters were at Méaulte.

8 October: From Albert we marched to Méaulte, entrained from there on the newly made railway to Mametz Wood (between Fricourt and Mametz Wood, Bottom Wood near Fricourt) and after a fearful march over really muddy roads, we went into trenches opposite the Butte de Warlencourt and Eaucourt l'Abbé. Here we relieved the 47th (London) Division. I call them trenches but that is hardly the word. But we knew by this time what our newly captured positions were. They were hovels of the perfectly thick mud variety. Mud and bodies were the orders of the day. Stacks of unburied dead, Highlanders and others. And the smell!

We landed into this in the middle of the night after a shelly walk and so next day we spent in counting up our losses and digging our holes in the side of the trench. Everything had been done in such a hurry that we were perfectly sure we should not see our rations as our transport had been left in Albert. So we lived on what we had carried up.

All that day we spent in looking at the land around as we had been informed that we were to capture the Butte de Warlencourt, a real machine-gun nest, two days later. 'B' Company was to lead the way.

None of us relished the idea as we were relying on the support of the 47th Division Artillery.

9 October: Next morning, just after dawn, I was passing along our so-called trench to see the Division on our right when I received my wound. A German flare light, which had been picked up in the trenches, was accidentally discharged and I took the discharge at close quarters. In the best of places such a thing would be inconvenient, but here of all spots it was horrible.

My left leg was badly burnt from the thigh to the knee and I suffered considerably from shock. This and the mud set me running. It was with great difficulty that our company stretcher bearers (can I ever forget Robinson) held me down and carted me off to the MO's dug-out. He, (Millerick by name) patched me up as best he could and I continued the painful journey on stretcher to the first aid station at Bazentin. Here I received an injection which eased matters. From there in a jolty Ford ambulance to the Corps dressing station at Bécourt. Thence by the same car to the CCS at Dernancourt. Here my servant Neil, who had accompanied me, left.

To Mrs Edith Weir   *Dernancourt Casualty Clearing Station*
                                        [Wednesday] 11 October 1916

My Dear Mother,

Just a line to say I was wounded by a rocket light yesterday. My leg is burnt from the knee up to the thigh. I go down to the base today, but I don't expect it is bad enough to get to Blighty with. Perhaps it is all for the best as we were just going to have another 'go'.

I will let you know my new address.

Yours,
Neil

War Diary   October 1916

I spent a few days [at Bernancourt] and painful ones they were. Then I was sent down by ambulance train to Rouen, where I was lodged in No. 8 Base Hospital. This train journey was like a funeral. We took nineteen hours to get to Amiens and another ten hours to get from there to Rouen.

The Base Hospital was equally unpleasant. All sorts of painful dressings were applied and they caused agonies to get off. The poor fellow in the bed next to me was off his head and at one period threatened to do me in.

To Mrs Edith Weir   *No. 8 Base Hospital, Rouen*
                                        [Friday] 13 October 1916

My Dear Mother,

My present address is No. 8 General Hosp[ital], Rouen. I hope to be in England in two or three days.

Yours with love,
Neil

War Diary   October 1916

From Rouen we trained to [Le] Havre, were put on board a hospital ship and sailed for Southampton. Thence to Oxford by quick train, where I arrived on October 17th. Here I was put in the leg ward of Somerville College Hospital for officers, which was attached to the 3rd Southern General Hospital.

From Military Secretary, War Office *to* Mrs Weir   *Telegram*
15 October 1916

Captain N. A. C. Weir, Argyll & Sutherland Highlanders, admitted 8 General Hospital, Rouen, October 13, with burn right thigh slight.

To Mrs Edith Weir   Somerville College Officers' Hospital, Oxford
[Tuesday] 17 October 1916

My Dear Mother,

Just a line to say I have arrived quite happily.

This Hospital is at Somerville College (the late Ladies College), just behind Keble. One of the nurses, a Miss Owen, knows all our part of the country very well. She often stays at Temple Laugherne with the Bests. She used to live in Grimley and is Harry Childens' niece.

Well you might easily train down one day and see me. I am very glad I got here.

> *Yours with love,*
> *Neil*

War Diary   October/November 1916

On examination my leg was found to be in a fearful state and very septic and the doctors advised amputation. Luckily a doctor named Wood applied the Ambrine Wax Treatment which was instrumental in saving the leg and causing much less pain.

From 'J. B.'   *10th Argylls, In the Field*
[Tuesday] 7 November 1916

Dear Sir,

I am sending 'B' Company casualties[1] with Mr Ramsay to post on arrival in England as it would probably get censored if sent otherwise. Hope you are speedily recovering from your injuries and able to be about by this time. We are having a sort of rest just now near the line, digging every day but not doing trench duty, in the vicinity of Arras at a village called Simencourt.

Mr Mackie was left in charge of the company when you came a cropper but took sick and has been in hospital since. We have a 2/Lt [second-

---

1. Most sustained in the attack on the Butte de Warlencourt on 10 November that Weir would have taken part in had he not been injured the day before.

lieutenant] i/c [in charge] of the company now, and are struggling to get the usual deficiencies made up. We got a draft of 52 to the company before they left Le Sars & Butte de Warlencourt trenches. They came from the 2/9th [Argylls]. We are settled down and have got the mud scrubbed off and enjoying the hardest rest we have had yet. Mr Andrews & Sergeant Marchbanks are on leave just now, and Mr Ramsay going today. I suppose you will know all the officer casualties in the Battalion from the papers, so am sending the company's only. We are expecting to move back a bit very shortly but probably it is one of the many rumours. Still it looks probable seeing the leave has started. Drop a P.C. [postcard] if you receive this all right. Can't think of anything else you would care to know. I hear Sergeant Henderson, Privates Sandilands & Robertson are being recommended for the Military Medal, not a bad pick I believe. All wish you to have a speedy recovery according to what I hear.

Yours very sincerely,

J. B.

Killed or Died of Wounds:

2nd Lt. Wilson,	*Pte. Rutherford, S.B. [stretcher-bearer]*
Pte. Balbirnie (8) [Platoon]	*Pte. Atchison (8) S.B.*
Pte. McConnachie (7)	*L/Cpl. Whyatt*
Pte. McNeill (trench mortar)	

Wounded:

Capt. Weir	*2nd Lt. McCallum*
L/Sgt. Shennan	*Pte. Finlayson*
Pte. Ross	*Pte. Ritchie*
Pte. Shannon	*Pte. Acton*
Pte. Brady	*Pte. Fleming*
Pte. McGovern	*Pte. McIntosh*
Pte. McSherry S.B.	*Pte. Travers*
Pte. Abernethy	*Pte. Coutts*
Pte. Innes	*Pte. McSweeney*
Pte. Micham	*Pte. Caskie*
Pte. Dayden	*Pte. Docherty*
L/Sgt. Wardrop	*Pte. Howie*
Pte. Wilson	*Pte Thomson*
L/Cpl. Thomson	

Missing:

Sgt. Sutherland	*Pte. McFarlane*
Pte. Waddell	*Pte. Farquharson*
Pte. McDonald	*Pte. Clark*

Also a good many went to hospital from exposure as it was terrible bad weather. The Battalion was the worst I have seen it up to the neck in mud.

From Lieutenant James Mackie   *OC 'B' Company, 10th Argylls,*
Canadian Convalescent Home for Officers,
Dieppe
[Thursday] 9 November 1916

My Dear Weir,
    Many thanks for your note of 27th October, which just arrived here a few minutes [ago] after having wandered over three quarters of France.
    Wilson was badly hit the day after you left, and McCallum was hit through the arm. Mac's was a 'cushy' one, but Wilson died at the CCS. Andrews had been sent down to the transport before the 'do', and came up during the night as I was left in sole possession of the line. After the 7th S[seaforths] & we were relieved by the other two batt[alions] of the Brigade, we had a few days back at High Wood, and then in, in support of a repetition of the same. I was suffering from bronchitis before I went in, and by the time I had been twelve hours in, the pain and the mud had developed what turned out to be an attack of PUO [pyrexia of unknown origin] or trench fever. I am convalescing here under very happy auspices.
    I don't know anything about Ramsay or Andrews. I haven't heard any news from the batt[alion] since I left. Sgt. Sutherland was missing believed wounded. Farquharson & Balbirnie were killed, and there were about fifty other casualties, the majority only slight. The other companies were less fortunate.
    I'd be very pleased to hear of your return to the battalion, as it is quite likely that we will be in a quieter place for a month or two to come.
    I expect to be back in the battalion within a week, so will keep you posted on Coy [Company] news.
    Best wishes.
                    Yours sincerely,
                    James Mackie

War Diary   November 1916

They were happy days in this hospital and Mother and Dorothy visited me,[1] as well as other friends.

---

1. In fact it was not until 13 November, more than three weeks after receiving her son's letter of 17 October, that Mrs Weir and her daughter Dorothy finally travelled to Oxford to visit Neil in hospital.

Diary of Mrs Edith Weir   November 1916

November 13th: Left Shrub Hill at 10:20 for Oxford, arrived 12:45 after slow but pleasant journey. Took bus to Axsuford Private Hotel – had some lunch and then to the Somerville Hospital to see Neil who is recovering from burns received on October 9th near Le Sars in the G[rea]t War. Poor boy, what sufferings he has gone through and so patiently too, but it is lovely to feel he is in England & safely out of the firing line for a bit. We found him wheeling himself about in a long invalid chair. 'Ben' [her dog] was not allowed in so had to be tied up to the doorstep, worse luck. Spent the afternoon mooning about the grounds and talking, & afterwards Dorothy went home for tea and I had a cup with Neil. He had a nice VAD Sister called Huxley who does not mind bringing in an extra cup and saucer. Left him about 5:30 and we spent the evening reading and working by the fireside. There are a number of Scotch ladies in the hotel.

November 14th: Fine but dull, spent the morning walking round the colleges & looking into the shops. Bought a pineapple to take to Neil. We all went to the hospital at 2:30 to take him out in a chair in the town. We first of all visited a shop to buy a cap. Poor boy, none of his kit has arrived yet. Then we went round by Keble and returned in time for tea. He said he enjoyed it, but I'm afraid the jolting was rather painful to his leg as the roads are none too well made. After dinner we went to a very gruesome show at one of the picture palaces. Bed a little after 10 p.m.

November 15th: Went shopping in the morning and chose a coat & skirt – in the afternoon took Neil out & we had tea at the Cadena Café. In the evening we worked & read in front of the fire.

November 16th: Walked around the Colleges in morning & did some shopping. A very cold wind blew. Took Neil out by St Barnabas Church and then back to the Cadena for tea where curiously enough we saw Mrs Blanch & Norman. The latter is in the RFA [Royal Field Artillery] & sails for India in a few days. Sat with Neil in his rooms till about 5:30 & then after dinner we went to the pictures at the North Oxford Cinema, 'Rupert of Hentzau' being the attraction.

November 17th: Town in morning – tried on coat & skirt. Very cold. Went to hospital at 2:30. Took Neil out but did not stay long as it was very cold. I had tea with him and D[orothy] went back to the Axsuford. Spent the evening talking round the fire.

November 18th: I went into town & Dorothy went to the station at 11.45 to meet Stuart Sheppard. A very cold wet morning, snow falling. They took a parcel of a cardigan for Neil to the hospital for me, then we had lunch & I went to the hospital to see Neil at the usual time. D[orothy] & Stuart visited a Lieut Morris who is in the Maitland Ward & after being wounded, started typhoid fever. Neil elected not to go out so Stuart & Dorothy went to Buols for tea & I stayed with him. After dinner at 6:30, we went to a cinema which S[tuart] had to leave at 9 o'clock to catch his train.

November 19th: Went round to hospital at 10 o'clock to take N[eil] to church but it was pelting so he decided not to venture out & we went to St Barnabas, very high ritual, to the High Celebration. Home for lunch and then afterwards we went to hospital. First of all visited Lieut Morris & then on to take Neil out. We came to the Axsuford for tea and he managed the steps on two sticks which is an improvement. Tea in the drawing room, which was not very lively, & then we took him back. Visited Mrs Dutteridge's husband who is in a ward with six other officers. After supper Dorothy's knitting caused much amusement!!

November 20th: Town in the morning & I bought a grey overcoat for it is very cold. I took some tickets to the stalls for the 5:30 performance of the Cinema Star which we hope Neil will be able to enjoy. Went to the hospital after lunch with Mrs Dutteridge & on the way D[orothy] and I paid another visit to Lieut Morris & took him some grapes. When we got to Neil's room we found Mrs D[utteridge] and her husband in it & they asked if they might borrow it for the afternoon if we were going out. Neil was waiting for us and went to the Cadena on sticks for the 1st time. Had tea, pretty music playing and then on to the theatre for the performance, which was not bad although it opened very tamely. Several other wounded officers there and one poor guy whom they have nicknamed the Cherub and is only 18½ & minus a leg amputated right up in the thigh - afterwards came to the Axsuford for dinner which they had kept for us & then Neil went back. Poor boy, he still looks very worn and pulled down. I suspect his first walk tired him out.

November 21st: Visited eleven of the Colleges in the morning. Worcester grounds very pretty & All Souls Chapel again. In afternoon went to hospital & Neil again came out on sticks & we proceeded slowly to the George Café for tea after doing a little shopping. Then went late to Cinema, but did not stay long. Walked back with Neil to hospital then home to the Axsuford for dinner - afterwards did our packing.

November 22nd: After breakfast, finished packing & ordered cab for 11:25 train. A beautiful morning & we are quite sorry to leave but must get home to prepare for Neil. Reached Shrub Hill 12:54 & Edwards Cab waiting for us which brought us to the cottage by 1:45. Stopped at the Cedars to get key of Fowl Pen. No deaths among the poultry this time & baby [*sic*] Robinson has looked after them very well. Unpacked & rearranged the house. Bill at hotel for nine days £6. 11. 4.

From Captain George Denham   *OC 'A' Company, 10th Argylls, BEF*
[Wednesday] 6 December 1916

My Dear Weir,

How are you getting on now after your unfortunate accident? I missed you a good deal and I hope when you are well enough we shall be lucky enough to get you back here again. We had a pretty dirty time at the Somme and were in some nasty corners. We were very unfortunate in losing dear old [Lieutenant] Russell [OC 'D' Company], and so many other officers & good NCOs. I was very lucky in my Co[mpan]y as Tully & I were the only officers wounded & mine was only a slight wound on the hand which did not interfere much. I am at the 3rd Army Infantry School at a captain's course and I return to the batt[alion] next Tuesday. It is a nice change here – there are twenty-four of us in this Mess and we are a cheery lot and have some jolly musical evenings. I wonder who will take over Windy Bill's [General Furse's] job now? We have a damned fine Brig.-General here as commandant – Solly-Flood.[1] Do you know him? With a bit of luck I hope to get some leave early next year. Well, Cheery-O, Weir, & all good wishes for a speedy recovery & a good good time.

Yours sincerely,
George Denham

War Diary   December 1916

The leg improved to such an extent that I was able to leave the hospital for home just before Christmas.

---

1. Later Major-General Sir Arthur Solly-Flood (1871–1940), Director of Training, BEF, January–October 1917 (when he helped to codify the British Army's tactical doctrine) and GOC 42nd Division, October 1917–November 1918.

10.

Service with an Officer Cadet Battalion

When Weir finally left hospital in December 1916, he was still 'very lame and could only get about with the aid of a stick'. As such he was unfit for active service (though he long hankered for a return to France) and instead was given the job of instructing future officers in an Officer Cadet Battalion (OCB), first in Oxford (where he was based, for a time, in his old college, Keble) and later at a newly formed battalion, the 21st, in Fleet near Aldershot.

Between August 1914 and March 1915, more than 20,000 temporary commissions had been granted to former members of the Officer Training Corps (OTC) like Weir. But in January 1915, with that reservoir all but emptied, the War Office decided to grant commissions to suitable men from the ranks. They were trained first by the OTC and, from February 1916, by the newly formed OCBs where a successful candidate would first have to complete a four-month course of instruction (later extended to five and then six months) that included, as Weir confirms, subjects as diverse as Tactics, Administration, Interior Economy, Map Reading, Military Law, Trench Warfare and Bombing, Drill, Physical Training and Bayonet Fighting. Many of the instructors were invalided veterans like Weir. In the summer of 1916 there were twelve OCBs; a year later that number had risen to twenty-three. By the end of the war they had trained more than 73,000 officers.

In all, Weir spent fifteen months as an OCB instructor, most of that time at Fleet where, in a curious echo of his time in the 10th Argylls, he first commanded a platoon and then a company. And all the time he kept up a constant correspondence with his former comrades in the 10th (some of whom had moved on to staff jobs) and the graduates of the OCB (many of whom were sent out to France). He even arranged for one old comrade, Captain Dick Knowling, MC (who had joined the 10th on the same day) to join the 21st OCB as a fellow officer instructor. Knowling later rejoined the 10th Argylls in France and was killed in action during the Ludendorff Offensive of late March 1918. (One of the most moving letters to Weir during this period was from Knowling's father, Jonathan, who wrote: 'It is difficult to realize that his soldier days are over; he was so keen on the work, but still, as he was originally intended for the army one must remember that his death in action is a fitting end to his career. He was so delighted on being able to get back to his old regiment & wrote very cheerily to the end.')

If the comments of his former cadets are anything to go by, Weir was an outstanding instructor whose platoons and companies generally swept the board of every competition they entered. He also made his mark as the officer in charge of shows and concerts. And yet Weir missed the comradeship of the 10th, if not the discomfort and danger of the front line, and made strenuous efforts to gain both a regular commission and a return to France. In neither was he successful, in the former case because no regular commissions were being given to those under the age of twenty-five (Weir was twenty-two on 25 April 1917).

His most faithful correspondent was Captain (later Major) W. S. Stevenson, DSO, MC, or 'Staggers' as Weir knew him, the former company commander and adjutant of the 10th who had since joined the staff of 15th Division. Other letter writers included Lieutenant Alick McCorquodale, his erstwhile platoon commander, who had since become aide-de-camp to his uncle General Horne, GOC First Army. It was from McCorquodale that Weir received the 'splendid news' of the Canadian Corps' capture of Vimy Ridge in early April 1917. From others he would hear word of the Étaples Mutiny and of the bloodbath that was Passchendaele or Third Ypres.

The Allied strategy for 1917 was the brainchild of General Robert Nivelle, the new French Commander-in-Chief, who had replaced Joffre in December 1916.

Nivelle's plan was for the French to land the main blow in Champagne, while British and French forces pinned German divisions in the Arras–Somme area. Specifically the BEF was to pierce the enemy positions, take the Hindenburg Line in the rear, and advance to Mons, Tournai and Courtrai. Further north, the British Second Army would exploit German weakness in Flanders and push forward.

The first BEF battle of 1917 was fought by the Fifth Army in January and February when it pushed five miles up the Ancre valley on a four-mile front. The Germans, planning a major withdrawal, were forced into a premature retreat in this sector. On 22 February the Germans began their planned move back to the Hindenburg Line, completing it by 28 March. The new German defences were based on an 'elastic' defence-in-depth. Attackers would need to fight through a lightly held outpost zone, intended to canalize them, before reaching the 'battle zone' of mutually supporting strongpoints, backed by further rearward defences. Disorganized by these defences, assault troops would be faced by *Eingreif* (counter-attack) divisions. Coming to terms with these new German tactics would be a major problem for the BEF in 1917.

The plan for the coming offensive was for General Allenby's Third Army to attack in the Arras sector, to capture 'the high ground about Monchy-le-Proux', and then, driving forward, to outflank the enemy defences to the south of Arras; meanwhile First Army (led by McCorquodale's uncle, General Horne) would assault the formidable Vimy Ridge. The BEF now had 1,157 heavy guns and at the beginning of the battle the density of heavy guns was about three times greater than at the equivalent stage of the Somme: 963 guns, or one per 21 yards, as opposed to 455, or one per 57 yards.[1]

The attack began on 9 April 1917 (Easter Monday) and was the BEF's most successful since the start of trench warfare. Lieutenant-General Sir Julian Byng's Canadian Corps (First Army) stormed Vimy Ridge. Meanwhile Third Army made deep inroads into Germany territory, with 9th (Scottish) Division advancing 3½ miles (hence Captain Stevenson's comment, in his letter of 12 August 1917, that 'Scotland can't do more') and another Kitchener division, the 12th, capturing enemy guns in Battery Valley. It demonstrated the huge strides the BEF had made in tactical proficiency.

The French offensive began on 15 April on the Chemin des Dames in Champagne (and continued until early May). It made moderate gains, but at a heavy cost, and triggered serious indiscipline in many French units (and led to Nivelle's replacement by Pétain on 15 May). 'At the end of May,' wrote Richard Watt, 'the troops that were revolting did not constitute a *revolutionary* force . . . Rather they were the symptoms of an almost mortal disease within the army: the disease of despair.'[2] Once conditions of service were improved – with better food, more regular leave and, most importantly, no more seemingly futile offensives, the loyalty of the French Army was never again in doubt. The perceived ringleaders, however, were harshly punished: 2,873 were convicted, 629 condemned to death and 43 actually shot;[3] hundreds of others, though reprieved, were sentenced to life imprisonment (with many selected for trial by their own officers and NCOs, with the implicit consent of the rank and file).

The consequence of the French mutinies for the BEF was that, henceforth, all major offensives would be undertaken by it alone. The statistics bear this out: the French Army suffered 306,000 fatalities in 1914; 334,000 in 1915; 217,000 in 1916; and 121,000 in 1917, mostly before the mutinies (giving a grand total of one million out of a male population of just 20 million).

By the summer of 1917, partly to distract attention from the stricken French Army, Haig was ready to attack in Flanders (an area of operations that he had long seen as offering the greatest opportunities for success). The first attack was at Messines, on the southern flank of the Ypres salient, on 7 June. It was undertaken by Plumer's Second Army which, in preparation,

---

1. Quoted in Sheffield, *The Chief*, p. 212.
2. Richard M. Watt, *Dare Call it Treason* (Simon & Schuster, 1995), pp. 195–6.
3. Stevenson, *1914–1918*, p. 328.

had dug twenty-one mines under the German lines and packed them with high explosive. The mines were detonated at 3 a.m., blowing off the crest of the ridge. Within hours the ridge had been captured. But when Plumer then asked for three days to prepare for a follow-up attack, Haig turned the operation over to Gough, who eventually advised against such an attack because it would result in 'a very difficult and exposed salient'.[1] Nevertheless the fighting was prolonged for a week and cost the British 25,000 casualties (and the Germans even more).

Haig immediately began to plan the main Ypres offensive and, as a year earlier, he had dual objectives: 'wearing out the Enemy' and 'securing the Belgian Coast and connecting with the Dutch frontier'. To achieve both he envisaged three phases: capturing the Passchendaele Ridge; moving on to Roulers; and an amphibious landing along the coast from Nieuport. 'If effectives or guns inadequate,' he wrote, 'it may be necessary to call a halt after No 1 is gained.'[2]

The offensive duly began on 31 July against the Gheluvelt plateau, south-east of Ypres, after a fifteen-day bombardment in which four million shells were fired. The attack was made by portions of the Second and Fifth Armies, supported by part of the First French Army on their left, and 136 tanks. Nine British divisions were involved (c. 100,000 men) and by the end of the day they had gained eighteen square miles for 27,000 casualties (the first day of the Somme, by contrast, had gained 3.5 square miles for twice the losses). Even so, the gains were far short of the day's objectives, despite advancing on a shorter front with air superiority and 48 tanks, and after firing four times as many shells.[3]

Gough captured the outlier known as Pilckem Ridge but not the Gheluvelt plateau. The weather then forced Gough to suspend operations until 16 August, when he tried another general offensive. It took the village of Langemarck on his left, but elsewhere counter-attacks nullified all the initial gains. At the end of the month Haig transferred the Gheluvelt plateau to the Second Army front and once more entrusted Plumer with principal responsibility for operations. Plumer, a prudent soldier with a competent staff, took three weeks to prepare, during which time the ground improved in an abnormally dry September. Then, in the three battles of the Menin Road (20 September), Polygon Wood (26 September) and Broodseinde (4 October), he largely achieved his limited objectives (advancing 1,000 yards over a narrow front) and beat off counter-attacks.

But Plumer became overconfident, leaving shorter intervals between each assault and less time to relocate his guns. In October heavy rain returned

---

1. Quoted in Sheffield, *The Chief*, p. 226.
2. Ibid., p. 227.
3. Stevenson, *1914–1918*, p. 334.

and two attacks towards Passchendaele ridge on the 9th and 12th were expensive failures. Haig should now have halted; but he insisted on carrying on, even when Gough wanted to stop. In successive bounds on 26 October, 6 and 10 November, the Canadian Corps finally took Passchendaele but suffered at least 12,000 casualties. By this stage the battlefield had become a wilderness of brimming shellholes, perilous duckboards, shattered forests, and obliterated villages.[1]

The capture of Passchendaele left the British less exposed to German gunfire and in command of most of the ridge, but the salient was deeper and more angular than in July and Haig admitted to General Sir William Robertson,[2] Chief of the Imperial General Staff (CIGS), that it would be untenable. The BEF had come nowhere near Roulers, still less the coast. Although the French had gained a breathing space, their chief protection was that the Germans never divined the extent of their mutinies and in any case did not intend a big offensive. Nor is it plausible, as it may be for the Somme, to argue that at least the British learnt something and improved their tactics. The BEF's effectiveness improved considerably in 1917, but not at Ypres. The British had lost 275,000 men; the Germans around 225,000.[3]

In early September 1917, while the fighting at Ypres was at its fiercest, a base camp at Étaples, near Boulogne, witnessed the war's only serious outbreak of disobedience by British and Empire troops (and one referred to by 'Witters', in his letter to Weir of 18 November, as 'some trouble they had with the Jocks'). The disorder was sparked on 9 September 1917 by the arrest and assault of a New Zealand gunner by the Military Police. It worsened when the outnumbered policemen shot into the angry crowd and killed a popular corporal of the Gordon Highlanders, prompting thousands of men to invade the town of Étaples in pursuit of the police. The unruly demonstrations continued for six days.

According to the camp adjutant, Major Guinness, the 'chief cause of discontent' was the fact that men who had already done much service at the front had to undergo 'the same strenuous training as the drafts of recruits arriving from home'. Guinness also referred to the lack of familiarity between officers and men: 'It should be realized that each Infantry Base Depot was commanded by an elderly retired officer who had an adjutant to help him. The remaining officers, like the men, were either reinforcements from home,

1. Ibid., pp. 335–6.
2. Later Field Marshal Sir William ('Wully') Robertson (1860–1933). The son of a Lincolnshire tailor, his rise from private soldier to field marshal is unique in the history of the British Army, and was thanks to keen intelligence, flair for languages and capacity for hard work. He had distinguished himself as Quartermaster-General of the BEF in 1914, particularly during the retreat to Mons, and was appointed CIGS in December 1915 to curb Lord Kitchener's power.
3. Stevenson, *1914–1918*, p. 336.

or had been sent down the line on account of ill-health, and therefore did not know them.'[1]

In their analysis of the disturbances, the historians Gill and Dallas referred to the 'particular hatred' directed towards the Military Police at Étaples – who had not seen active service and who were trying to impose 'the disciplinary standards of the glasshouse' – and the rioters' intention to release military prisoners. They also commented on the prominent role played by Anzac soldiers – who had a tendency to be 'contemptuous of the narrow discipline to which British soldiers subscribed, and [who] were led by officers who had invariably first shown their qualities as privates in the ranks' – and their close relationship with Scottish troops 'who gave the mutiny its force'. There was also the inevitable factor of low morale after three years of futile offensives.[2]

A number of men were charged with military offences, including Corporal Jesse Short of the Northumberland Fusiliers, who was found guilty of inciting his men to attack an officer (mutiny) and sentenced to death. Three other soldiers received 10 years' penal servitude, 10 were jailed for up to a year, 33 were given between 7 and 90 days field punishment and others were fined or reduced in rank. Short was executed by firing squad on 4 October 1917. Of the 53 men arrested, 18 were from Scottish battalions and 4 from Weir's former division, the 9th.[3]

Just as Weir was about to leave the 21st OCB in the spring of 1918 for, he hoped, a return to France, the Germans launched the first of a series of major offensives designed to end the war before the arrival of American troops (the United States had joined the Allies on 6 April 1917, but the bulk of their men would not reach the Western Front until 1918) tipped the balance against them.

The BEF was particularly vulnerable because its huge losses in 1917 (790,000 men) meant that it had to reduce the number of battalions in its divisions from twelve to nine. Among the battalions affected was Weir's old unit, the 10th Argylls, which was moved on 17 February from the 26th Brigade of the 9th (Scottish) Division to the 97th Brigade of the 32nd Division (much to the disgust of the serving and former soldiers of the 10th, Weir included). And yet each division still held the same length of front, so that the first line would have to be garrisoned more weakly or the infantry rotated out of it less frequently. Expecting an attack, Haig ordered the BEF to construct a system of defence in depth. It consisted of three zones: the forward zone, a 3,000-yard battle zone, and a rear zone four to eight miles behind it. The first zone, comprising 'outposts' rather than a continuous line of trenches, was to be held to the last man and in greater strength than by the Germans, and

---

1. Quoted in Douglas Gill and Gloden Dallas, 'Mutiny at Étaples Base in 1917', *Past and Present*, No. 69, 1975, pp. 97–8.
2. Ibid., pp. 98–102.
3. Julian Putkowski & Julian Sykes, *Shot at Dawn* (Pen & Sword, 1998).

the battle zone was to be rigidly held. Counter-attacks would be less speedy and automatic than under the German system, fewer response troops being stationed in the rearward area to deliver them and less discretion being delegated to their commanders.

The weakest-held sector was from Arras to St-Quentin where twelve divisions of Gough's Fifth Army were defending more than forty miles of front. This was deliberate. 'Of course I am uneasy,' Haig admitted, 'but where else can I afford to bend without risk of losing the war?'[1] His compromise was an agreement with Pétain, the French Commander-in-Chief, that the French would either take over a portion of the Fifth Army's line or reinforce it with six division if it were attacked; Haig agreed to do likewise.

The first German attack (Operation 'Michael') was launched on 21 March over a 50-mile front by 32 German divisions (with another 30 or so in reserve) after 6,473 guns had fired a five-hour barrage of 1.16 million shells. That day the Germans advanced up to 8 miles and took 98.5 square miles of territory (as much as the Allies had gained in 140 days on the Somme). German losses were 40,000 men; the British lost about the same (including 21,000 POWs) and also 500 guns. Everywhere the Germans overran the British forward zone, and along the southern quarter of the front (held by the Fifth Army) they got through the battle zone too. A dense fog assisted their advance. That evening, Gough ordered the Fifth Army to make a general retreat behind the Somme and Crozat canal.[2]

The Third Army, by contrast, held better-prepared positions with fewer men in the forward zone; but by delaying the progress of the German attack in the north it opened a gap between the two armies. By 23 March the Germans had created a forty-mile hole into open country. That day the first French troops arrived to help the BEF, and the 88,000 British troops on leave, as well as the mobile reserve, were rushed across the Channel and thrown into the fray. Even so contact between the British and French armies was almost lost as the German advance continued and, refusing to send more divisions to Haig's assistance, Pétain explained that his priority was to protect Paris and not the British flank.

The deadlock was broken when Haig agreed to subordinate himself to a French generalissimo in order to get extra French divisions north of the Somme. At a meeting of senior Allied politicians and generals at Doullens on 26 March, it was agreed to place Marshal Foch in overall command 'for the co-ordination of the action of the Allied armies on the Western Front', with Haig and Pétain remaining responsible for the tactical direction of their armies.[3]

---

1. Quoted in Sheffield, *The Chief*, p. 261.
2. Stevenson, *1914–1918*, pp. 408–9.
3. Quoted in Stevenson, *1914–1918*, p. 410.

The new arrangement helped to stem the tide, though the German attack was already running out of steam and was called off entirely on 4–5 April. Nevertheless, Ludendorff had done enormous damage, capturing 90,000 prisoners and 1,300 guns, and killing or wounding 212,000 Allied troops (including Weir's old comrade, Dick Knowling), although his own dead and wounded numbered 239,000. By the end of the battle, Haig had committed 48 of his 56 divisions, and the French a total of 40; by 3 April Haig had just one division in reserve.[1]

The second German offensive ('Georgette') was launched on the River Lys in Flanders on 9 April on a 20-mile front with 12 assault divisions (and 27 in all). Opposing them were just six British divisions and two Portuguese. By 12 April the Germans had again been able to break through on a front of 30 miles, forcing the British to evacuate their dearly won gains in the Ypres salient and withdraw to the gates of the city. Haig issued his famous 'backs to the wall' order. Yet by 18 April reinforcements had re-established the line. The last assault on 29 April – the day Weir joined the 3rd Argylls – was repelled by French troops that Foch had released from the general reserve. The Germans were stopped just five miles from the crucial railway junction at Hazebrouck, having inflicted 146,000 Allied casualties for 109,000 of their own.[2]

War Diary   January–April 1917

First of all I must say how I became attached to an Officer Cadet Battalion or an OCB as they are more generally known.

When I was in hospital at Oxford my old tutor at Keble College, Freddie Matheson by name, came to visit me. During the visit he asked me whether I felt keen on a job of instructing men to become officers and I must say that although I thought I should like the job I felt that I had no experience in that line. This however was one of the common errors that temporary officers made because when you take over a job in the Army it does not necessarily mean that you know anything about that job. Nevertheless he mentioned my name to Captain H. H. Hardy at the War Office, whose business it was to find suitable officers to act as instructors. He wrote to me saying that I should go and see him personally when I came out of hospital. This I did on 28th December 1916 and he told me that I should be appointed to an OCB when I was fit as I was then on eight weeks' leave.

Shortly after Colonel Stenning, commanding the 4th OCB at Oxford, wrote me suggesting that I should join his Battalion for the purpose of

---

1. Stevenson, *1914–1918*, p. 412.
2. Ibid., pp. 412–14.

looking round and getting into the run of things. Consequently I went up to Oxford on Jan. 24th, 1917 after I had had a medical board at Norton Barracks. I was still very lame and could only get about with the aid of a stick. Colonel Stenning attached me to his 'D' Company who were in Wadham College and under the command of Major Maule of the Essex Regiment. And I soon found out what little I knew and how rusty I was. I suppose it was after service in France.

Three days later I was transferred to Freddie Matheson's Company ('C') at Keble and I found myself once more back in the old college, but this time living in the guest room and feeding with the dons in the SCR [Senior Common Room] as the other instructors did. Amongst them were Calf, Newman, Keble and King, all old Keble men.

On February 4th Captain Hardy came down to pay us a visit and asked me if I should like to go down to a newly formed OCB at Fleet, near Aldershot. If so I should start by acting as Adjutant and should write to Lieutenant-Colonel G. F. H. Dickson (Royal Welsh Fusiliers) who was in command. This I did and received orders to report there on February 7th.

The 21st OCB was then being formed and the huts at our camp were still occupied by the RAMC depot who were leaving in drafts. Colonel Dickson had only four officers including the Quartermaster and about a dozen or so men to perform a permanent staff with the prospect of the arrival of 300 cadets the following day.

Thus there was no time for words and I had to get down to it and try to form an orderly room with the aid of an ex-Lewis gun corporal. It was an uphill task and all the more so for me as I had no experience in this line before. There were no chairs, tables, stationery etc. In fact the whole thing was in a glorious muddle and well-nigh sent the Colonel off his head.

The Colonel kindly let me sleep in his room in camp and have the use of his servant, Pte Matheson of the 5th Argyll & Sutherland Highlanders. I felt very miserable and the Mess was chaotic.

On the 8th the 300 Cadets arrived and were formed into 'A' & 'B' Company under Major S. J. M. Sampson (London Regiment) and Major F. C. Finch (Gloucester Regiment).

My time as Adjutant was spent in trying to get straight, writing out orders (as there were no typewriters), interviewing all sorts of people (chiefly tailors), and visiting Aldershot Command Headquarters with the Colonel trying to get men for the permanent staff.

Soon a second-in-command, Major Green of the Devonshire Regiment, and a Parade Adjutant, Captain C. B. Jones of the Northumberland Fusiliers, turned up.

We gradually got rid of the RAMC and things began to settle down. The cadets had a rough time of it and instruction was very elementary but they made the best of it. Their feeding arrangements were none too good owing to a bad Administrative Officer and quarrels between the Army Canteens and Women's Legion. Everyone was pretty unhappy.

On February 13th, the Adjutant, Captain R. B. Corser, Yorkshire Regiment, arrived and I handed over in a fairly straight condition and was posted to 'B' Company. But before that I was offered the post of Administrative Officer, but no thank you!

Captain (later Major) Finch put me in charge of No. 8 Platoon (the Jock Platoon) and I was also second-in-command of the Company. Our other officers were Lieutenant Oliver, DLI, with No. 6 Platoon and Lieutenant J. M. Muir (Gordon Highlanders) with No. 5 Platoon. Our training chiefly consisted of PT and drill under the cadets themselves as we had no NCO instructors.

Thus really the first month was wasted settling down, but officers & NCOs gradually turned up and amongst them Lieutenant R. J. Booth, London Regiment, an excellent Administrative Officer. Lieutenant R. A. Angier, Gloucestershire Regiment, joined and took over No. 6 from Oliver who went to the newly formed 'C' Company (Capt. J. S. Davenport, Bedfordshire Regt.). Lieutenant M. Gordon, Worcestershire Regiment, took over No. 7 Platoon.

At the beginning of each month new companies were formed:- 'D' Company under Major J. M. Wadmore, Inniskilling Fusiliers, and 'E' Company under Captain C. S. Fuller, East Surrey Regiment. I mentioned Dick Knowling's name to the Colonel and he joined us and was posted to 'E' Company. The first course, which lasted four months, was carried out according to the War Office programme. The Colonel was madly keen on inter-platoon competitions and when the officers presented the Battalion with a fine cup, he inaugurated one cup competition at the end of each month. Military subjects alone were taken as:- Physical Training & BF [Bayonet Fighting], Drill, Musketry Rapid Fire, Assault Course Practice, Rifle v Bayonet etc. Everyone got mad keen to win that cup and practised out of hours at these various subjects. The Jocks were extra special and carried off the first competition for 'B' Company after defeating the Jock Platoon (No. 4) of 'A' Company. These competitions fostered a healthy rivalry amongst the cadets and they were conducted with the utmost fairness as all the judges came from outside the unit.

Now back to our training. It was considered that you could get the best out of the instructors if each took his special subject. This was hardly the War Office view as they wished an instructor to teach all subjects. This was hardly feasible and so we divided our subjects as follows:- Finch took Tactics and Administration, Angier took Map Reading, Gordon took Law, Muir took Lewis Gun and Gas, while I took Trench Warfare and Bombing.

During the course we were visited by General Sir Archibald Hunter, the GOC Aldershot Command, Brigadier-General Gordon, Deputy Director of Staff Duties, and Brigadier-General A. J. Chapman, Inspector of Infantry. Colonel Dickson also arranged for officers of the Senior Officers' School under General Kentish and officers of the various army schools to visit. These visits were afterwards elaborated and these officers spent two or three days with the various companies and followed out their system of training. How smart the cadets looked when the got their cadet uniform, which was made by Messrs. Alderton and Co., Strand. Colonel Dickson was so very particular as regards their turn-out and he made arrangements to see each uniform fitted. Rightly so, and not only did the cadets look smarter than those of other cadet battalions but the cadet uniform allowance was properly spent.

I suppose that one of the features of the 1st and 2nd Courses were the various stunt exhibitions that were given in Drill, BF & Physical Training etc. to those institutions that were fortunate enough to see them. This had the detrimental effect from the cadets' point of view of taking them away from their officer instructors and stuffing them under the NCO instructors. Consequently Map-Reading and Tactics suffered.

Personally I found my Company Commander hard to work with and probably the fact that he lived out had something to do with it.

Now as to games. 'A' & 'B' Companies held sports on the race-courses and Cadet Harvey of No. 8 Platoon won the individual cup. We also got up concerts in the big hall. I was OC [of Entertainments] in the Battalion. Newman of 'A' Company was very energetic and produced the 'Country Girl' in an open air theatre. It was a great show.

This opera was a successful wind-up to our first course.

The first course was not a great success. We had a very bad start and the instructors were not used to this special work. Luckily the cadets were a clever lot and in most cases passed their War Office examinations, which papers the instructors had to correct. We were sorry to lose a sporting lot, who had plenty of 'esprit de corps' and I was especially sorry to lose my fine Jock Platoon.

The Battalion second-in-command, Major Green, left and was succeeded by Major C. R. B. Henderson of the Black Watch.

From **Captain W. S. Stevenson**   *9th Divisional Staff*
                                                         20 March 1917

Dear Weary,

Here we are again! Rosie [Cavendish] is sitting here beside me, as he is in the Brigade Office having got the job as learner to the Brigade-Major which the General wanted to give to you, only malheureusement, you had all departed.

I had a letter from Currie the other day. He is now with the 3rd Battalion with Davidson and Ian Stewart and Tweedie. Dick [Knowling] has been sent across to Dunfermline to the Training Reserve. Also he is engaged to be married, according to a Times announcement of a recent date!

Ned MacMillan got hit again the other day, in the head but not seriously. We went to see him at the F[ield] A[mbulance] before he was evacuated, and he was very cheery and said he was off to Blighty to be Dick's best man.

The Regiment are having sports the day after tomorrow. The chief item of interest is a high jumping competition between [Captains] French and McQueen, for a vast wager of fifty francs! Each rather fancies his chances, but the betting is rather in favour of McQueen, partly on account of French's dicky knee and partly from a rumour (started I believe by McQ himself) that he was once known to clear 5' 3"!

Johnny D[ashwood] is somewhere round here but, though we sent the most appealing messages to him, by every Tank fellow we see, he hasn't been over to see us so far.

I see you now have the 'paper' job for which your soul used to yearn. I hope it doesn't arise and smite you so that you may wish you are once again commanding Bluggy B in 47S.[1]

I hope you are off light duty now and that your legs are all right again. Rosey has a servant from 'B' called O'Brien and he was lamenting the other day that you didn't go home with a decent wound, so you see how they all had your interests at heart.

Are you really an Englishman! What a confession after all the scraps we had on the subject, or are you only pulling my leg once again.

I'll send you one of these photos when they arrive. I expect you'll bung it among your papers, so that no one may suspect you of harbouring in your heart the dreadful secret that you receive letters from one whose name is on the roll of shame.

Write me again soon, as I must 'keep touch'. By gad we've had to keep touch on some funny occasions haven't we? I shall always remember

---

1. A tumble-down trench in the Ypres salient that Weir described as the 'worst' he experienced.

your fitting acknowledgements at Montauban – your Oo No – received, thank the Lord! That went into the War Diary.

Don't expect any war news from me. I never write any; the home papers always know more and besides I'm too close to it to be really interested.

Cheer-oh, old thing.

Yours,
Staggers

From Lieutenant Alick McCorquodale

HQ First Army
16 April 1917

Dear Weir,

How nice of you to write me. Thank you so much. Have been on this job now since January [ADC to his uncle General Horne, GOC First Army]. It isn't a bad job, but you get damned fed up with it and I expect I shall be back with the battalion again some day, and perhaps have the luck to be in your Company. Splendid news out here now.[1] I went all over the captured Vimy Ridge three days ago. Up to our new line the place is in an awful mess. I saw our old bit place in the line near the Burrows looking alright! Mackenzie is an old friend of mine and a very nice chap indeed. I saw George Crichton in turn about a month ago, in Carlton House Terrace, and was round at his house often with his sisters! God knows when I shall get leave again, probably about next October I should think. So glad you are enjoying yourself and congratulations about your platoon, also many congratulations on getting the MC.[2] Hoping to hear from you again soon. I see by the papers that Patterson is wounded again. Goodbye & Good luck.

Yours ever,
Alick McCorquodale

From Lieutenant Alfred D. Duff[3]

19 Leslie Street,
Pollokshields, Glasgow
16 May 1917

My Dear Weir,

This is a somewhat belated reply to yours of Easter Day, and the only excuse I have to plead is the usual one, procrastinating.

---

1. Canadian troops of Horne's First Army captured the important Vimy Ridge in Artois on 12 April 1917 after four days of fighting and 11,000 casualties. The Canadians won four VCs.

2. Weir never received the Military Cross, though it was the least he deserved for his work on the Somme.

3. Duff had joined 'B' Company, 10th Argylls, as a 2nd lieutenant in October 1915. He lost

I was right glad to hear from you again. It was like a voice out of the past: for somehow since poor old [Lieutenant] Dickerson [OC 6 Platoon, 'B' Company] went [killed during the attack on Longueval on 14 July 1916] I've lost touch with the 10th altogether. As for [Lieutenant R.] Thomson, I've never seen or heard anything about him since his return to Blighty.

Well I'm glad you have a cushy job now in England, and I'm sure you won't mind if it's for the duration. As for myself, I have not yet been officially discharged, though that was recommended about three and a half months ago. They've given me a gratuity of £250, and a pension of £100, so that's not bad, and meantime my pay is going on as well, so under the circumstances I don't mind if they forget about my discharge a little longer. However, all that doesn't prevent my carrying on my own line. I finished off my college course last December, and am now 'The Rev.', and since the beginning of the year I've been assistant in one of the city churches here and having a fairly decent time. However I want to get a nice little country job, and am keeping my eyes open, and I hope to be able to get settled before very long.

As for my health, I'm feeling pretty fit now, and getting on wonderfully with the one paw. Of course I would prefer to have another one, but I'm right glad to be just as I am. I have applied to get into Roehampton[1] but there are a hundred or so before me, so it may be a month or two yet before I get there. When I do come south, we must arrange to have a night together for old time's sake. So if you leave Hants. let me know your change of address, and I'll let you know when I'm coming.

Cheero.

> Yours,
> Alfred D. Duff

War Diary   May 1917

The second course started off with a tremendous flare. We had the same officers with the exception of Angier who had gone off to get married so 'B' Company received the additional assistance of Major A. L. Ashwell, DSO, of the Sherwood Foresters. As he was only with us for a short time I was still second-in-command and OC No. 8 Platoon, another Jock Platoon.

------

an arm to an accident on a trench mortar course at the Second Army School in May 1916 and was invalided home.

1. Queen Mary's Hospital, Roehampton, was set up in 1915 as a specialist centre for fitting prosthetic limbs. More than 41,000 British soldiers lost limbs during the First World War, a relatively low figure helped by the introduction in 1916 of the Thomas Splint which immobilized compound fractures and allowed them to heal.

But this time everything was cut and dried. We started our syllabus right away and we had the glorious weather of June. Booth's messing arrangements were A1 and the WAACs worked with a will. The first thing we did was to get the company rigged out in gym vests of blue and red (Guards colours) with a big 'B' on the chest. We also started a Company shield competition.

Stunts and exhibitions were still going strong and on July 24th we were honored by a visit from their Majesties the King and Queen accompanied by the Princess Mary and Duke of Connaught.

To Mrs Edith Weir

Staff Mess, Crookham, Fleet
26 July 1917

My Dear Mother,
The King, Queen, Princess Mary and Duke of Connaught came down to see us at work the evening before last. We are out on the rifle range the whole of this week – a wretched business. I go to a two day's gas course tomorrow.

Mr Attwood wants me to go to Scotland on my next leave, which starts on Friday week. I doubt if it will come off.
Yours,
Neil

From 2nd Lieutenant John Bascenden

10th Scottish Rifles,
20 Infantry Base Depot,
Étaples, northern France
9 August 1917

Dear Weir,
Just a word as to how a few of your old platoon are going on. You see I have arrived once more in the 'Sunny Land' [France] and have already thought it better to be in No. 8 Platoon as a cadet than to be in the 'bull ring' at the Base.[1] *A huge crowd of us came over here last Friday and I have met several 21 OCB folks from both 'A' & 'B' Co[mpan]ys and apart from the 'bull ring' training we are having a rare old time.*

Cunningham, Simpson G. P., McHail, McDougall, Matheson, Sayers, Martin, McClintock & several more are here so the two 'Jock' platoons are well represented. We still tease the No. 4 [Platoon] men about the competitions.

---

1. 20 Infantry Base Depot, Étaples, northern France, the location for the infamous 'mutiny' in September 1917.

*As regards postings, Cunningham is for the 17th HLI along with
Martin (No. 4) and McClintock, Matheson & McHail are for the 16th RS.
McDougall is for the 9th Seaforths, Sayers the 9th SR and Simpson &
myself for my old battalion, the 10th Scottish Rifles.*

*I suppose the wheel of change will be going round at Twezeldown
[camp] - with new cadets rolling up & out. Have you had any more
productions like 'French as he is spoke'? McHail often speaks of it. One
gets the real thing hereabouts.*

*Please give all our kind regards to the officers & tell Cap[tain] Jones
that No. 8 is still going strong & give Major Finch our congrats on his
majority & accept from me on behalf of the others our kindest regards.*

Yours sincerely,

John Bascenden

From **Captain W. S. Stevenson**   *9th Divisional Staff, BEF*

22 August 1917

Dear Weary,

*The General has gone on leave and he asked me to tell you about your
application for a permanent commission.*

*I enquired at the Division and they showed me a memo in which
it was laid down definitely that no applications would be considered
from officers under 25 years of age. So I'm afraid that's that. The only
thing to do now is to apply on AF [Army Form] MT 315A and ask that
your commission be antedated to 9 months subsequent to your first
commission i.e. about 24 May 1915 if you had attained the age of 19 on
that date.*

*That's what Rosy Cavendish did, only he has just applied now to have
it antedated. At present he appears in the Army List as a 2nd Lt in the
Sherwood Foresters dated 4 January 1917 or thereabouts.*

*Rosy and I are coming on leave in a day or two. He'll be at Eaton Rise,
Ealing. I'll be God knows where as I'm going to be married.*

*Now let me answer my letter from you dated 24th March 1917 - a lot
has happened since then. I suppose you've noticed about the casualties in
the Scottish regiments and at the same time read the gup about Canada
at Vimy [Ridge] and Australia at Bullecourt and the 'county regiments'
in front of Arras.*

*One would think poor old Scotland had done nothing, instead of
having three divisions in[,] all of which have done extraordinary work,
which the Boche knows much better than the people at home. Scotland
can't do more and all the men are fighting, most of them have fought in
fact, that is their fighting is over for they're dead.*

If you put it into Latin you may understand pugnaverunt – they have finished with fighting.

I say, Weary, do you sing 'All dressed up' at those concerts of yours? I hope you do. It must be a scream.

I believe Dick [Knowling] is with you now, isn't he? Give him my love and tell him W. St Clair Grant of the Camerons is staying at the Langham [Hotel] till about the 31st if he wants to see him. They are both engaged too – what lads we are to be sure.

Tiny Taylor is out again – he was FOO [Forward Observation Officer] to A&SH [Argyll & Sutherland Highlanders] in the last strafe and practically filled the dug-out.

We're still a cheery party – McQueen, Cavendish, Bonnyman, Archie, self and French. Poor old Colvin has gone west – sniped in the last show.

If you want to see me badly send a wire to 9 Hoswell Road, Muswell Hill, N.1, and say when you can get away and I'll tell you where I'll be if I can.

Cheerio,
Staggers

War Diary   August–December 1917

Soon [after the visit from the King and Queen], General Sir William Robertson spent a day with us. Angier returned and the course proceeded on its way. I found it more difficult to work with Finch as he was not over keen on giving detailed orders. My position therefore was an unenviable one.

Colonel Dickson presented the Battalion with a fine cup which was held by the best all round company. Not only did 'B' Company win it but No. 8 Platoon won the Inter-Platoon Cup and Company Shield so we didn't do badly.

How jealous the other companies were.

Games were a great success with Knowling as Battalion Games Officer. Tennis was played on the Fleet tennis ground and proved to be most popular. Certainly the courts were good.

Each company took upon itself to give a goodbye treat to the rest of the Battalion on its leaving.

'C' Company gave some excellent sports on the race course ices galore.

'D' Company gave a regatta on Fleet Canal.

'E' Company got down some stars from town to give an open-air concert. They included Violet Loraine, Phyllis Monkman and Jack Buchanan.

'A' Company gave a torchlit tattoo and 'B' Company gave their celebrated revue entitled 'What ho, Pyramids!' in the big riding school.

Two thousand people witnessed the revue which was written by the cadets themselves. The scenery was also painted by cadets and the cast numbered nearly fifty. I took the part of Little Freddie.

And so our second course ended towards the close of September and we parted sorrowfully from a good all round company.

The cadets were a pleasanter crowd than the first lot but they did not know as much. However we taught them more.

It was unfortunate that Angier got scarlet fever and so he was away for most of the course. His place was filled by Champion of 'E' Company. In the Mess, affairs were rather strained between the officers of the 20th & 21st OCBs. The Colonels did not really hit it off.

Our third course opened with great changes. First of all Colonel Dickson left and was succeeded by Lieutenant-Colonel H. W. Smith, DSO, of the Queen's [Regiment]. Colonel Smith had previously been an instructor at the RMC in pre-war days, and during the war he was commandant of the General Headquarters Cadet School at St-Omer. Naturally he made gradual changes. So not much attention was paid to Drill & Physical Training but more to the thinking side of the training. Games were also boomed [*sic*]. It thus took the officers a little more time to get into the new regime and now they were actually given a free hand with which to carry out their ideas. Finch and Davenport both left, while Ashwell and I took over their respective companies. I did not find it hard to take over the Company as I had to do most of the running of it when Finch was there. He was an extremely nice man but was not endowed with a soldier spirit. [C. B.] Jones, the Parade Adjutant, also left and soon after old Corser, the Adjutant, was succeeded by Gaskell of 'C' Company.

'B' Company itself consisted of Lancashire products and I missed my Jocks. I think that the Lancashire people are hard to deal with. Amongst the officers, Muir was lent to 'A' Company and Usher, a great gas expert, replaced him. Usher's health was none too good. He suffered fearfully from fever. Hunt, a ranker officer of the King's and a good fellow, replaced me at No 8. Angier, who was now living out, had the most chronic rheumatism, so we were really rather a lot of crocks!

I now instructed in Tactics, Administration and Interior Economy. The War Office increased the length of the course to five months and a fresh syllabus was issued – a good thing.

Things went along very smoothly and Colonel Smith's methods made it considerably easier for the instructors. He always kept a kind eye on us.

The Company and Platoon Cup competitions were abolished, but the 'Incubator', our local paper, gave a Games Cup.

I must tell you about the 'Incubator'. Originally the 20th and 21st OCBs amalgamated and edited a paper called the 'White Band'. However there was some hitch and so we started one of our own by name 'The Incubator'. It was a great success and edited by Skevington of 'E' Company.

Games were then on the ascendant and needless to say 'B' Company won the games cup too. We had a good rugger team, soccer team and hockey team. Our running was weak.

Teams also represented the Battalion and we played the RMC etc. Most of the Officers played Hockey under Knowling's captaincy and we had some real good matches especially the RMA one when we had a night in town. We beat the RMA & RMC. I played outside left.

Concerts were not encouraged but each platoon gave one and we gave a good end of course one in the big hall.

'B' Company also inaugurated a debating society, much to the amusement of the other companies.

Now as to changes, Major Henderson was replaced by Major H. St. J. Jefferies, DSO, Worcestershire Regiment as second-in-command. Knowling left for France.

From 2nd Lieutenant John Bascenden

Somerville Hospital,
Oxford
20 October 1917

My Dear Weir,

Very many thanks for your letter which has at last reached me, and very many hearty congrats on the success of No. 8 [Platoon]. I suppose you have won the cup outright now. It is really remarkable such success and speaks volumes for the OC Platoon [Weir].

You will wonder at the above address. An accident in the front line in front of Monchy (where we had gone after a few stints at Ypres) sent me here. I had an operation on October 2nd and in another three weeks will be GS [fit for General Service]. Harrison of 'A' Co[mpan]y is here too.

Yes, No. 8 seem to have had a pretty bad time. Loring (you remember the Scots Guards fellow) who was with McHail in the 16th RS has lost his sight I fear.

I think the 21st is known pretty well as 'some' OCB. There are lots of cadets in Oxford but they lack the Cappy Jones[1] touch.

Hope your orders for Folkestone do not arrive.

Kind regards,

Yours sincerely,
John Bascenden

---

1. Captain Jones, the Parade Adjutant at 21st OCB.

From 'Witters'[1]

46 Queen's Road, Tunbridge Wells
18 November 1917

My Dear old Natters,

I have often wondered what you are doing nowadays and am very sorry I have not tried to find out before but somehow or other I have not seemed to find time to do so. I got your letter last April when I was going out with my division; owing to some really shady work at the War Office we were kept back, and a month ago the division was split up and sent across in drafts; we left our men at the Base at Étaples after having been with them since Nov. 1914.

The officers are going out in pairs and I go on Tuesday week. My young brother who was in Eton collars at Tonbridge when I was gazetted has been out with the RFA since last March.

They tell me I shall be sent to one of my own battalions but I doubt it as I have been signalling officer since 1915 so shall have to go where required. Well old thing that describes my inglorious service up to the present date; I am not a scrimshanker though it must look remarkably like it but if you ever run up against any other poor blighter in the 67th Division he will tell you the same.

I have not much news of the old crowd; I heard from the Dean [of Keble College] about two months ago; of course you heard of his DSO – got a chunk taken out of his head so he says. By the way many congratters on your mention [in despatches][2] – I saw it in the last Keble list.

I have been doing some Signal work with some Camerons lately who knew Cameron of Keble; he was their Signalling Officer; they told me he was caught by a direct shell at Loos: apparently he meant to stick to the Army as a Chaplain after the war.

When I was sitting in the Officers' Mess at Étaples I heard someone shout out for Captain —— (I didn't catch his name) of the 10th A & S Highlanders; of course I nipped after him as I thought he could tell me something of you but unfortunately I could not reach him as he dashed out to stop some trouble they had with the Jocks just then – in fact they had wind up pretty badly over it. He was a thickset fellow with auburn hair and one wound stripe. A fellow was attached to our crowd who was a cadet at Keble and by a great coincidence had my old rooms P.II. He told me that all our furniture was put in the bedders [bedroom] and the sitter [sitting-room] was handed over to the Cadets.

---

1. Unidentified.

2. Temporary Captain N. A. C. Weir was mentioned in a Despatch from General Sir Douglas Haig, dated 13 November 1916, 'for gallant and distinguished services in the Field'. It entitled him to wear an oak leaf on his uniform.

I have to come up to town on Wednesday next; if you chance to be anywhere near there on that day I could meet you at any time after 12 anywhere you liked to name. If you are still at the OCB at Fleet you could come back fairly easily.

However I suppose this is one of the possible pleasures of life that don't come off and must wait till the end of the war.

Cheero and let me have a line some time to say you are still alive.

As ever,
Witters

From Captain C. B. Jones

NCO School, Tidworth, Hampshire
11 December 1917

My Dear Weir,

Thank you so much for your letter & news therein. Sorry I haven't answered before but have just returned from a tour round the Southern Command schools, spending last week round at the Bombing School, Lyndhurst, Southampton.

Well I have settled here but am a proper round peg in a square hole, for they don't know what to do with me for as soon as I came I got the CO to forward an application to get me to France, so am just waiting orders.

This week I started a two week course of boxing, wrestling & football, which takes place at the Garrison Gym here, the object being that it is taught in Regts & schools instead of PT. So am passing the time away fairly pleasantly.

I understand things are slightly altered in the good old Batt[alion]. I have met many people here who visited the Batt[alion] and one and all are quite full of France and say they have yet to see a show to beat [Third Ypres]. So much for our fame.

I should be delighted to hear you had got the BB ['Blubby B'?] Troop, for no one knows better than yourself to whom the credits of their past successes are due to. And successes of the autumn I hope.

My bike, I understand, is in the shed and I am asking £15 for it, so if you come across anyone who requires one or will make a bid for it you will do me a favour, for it's rather a white elephant at present.

I regret not having any photos with me but am in hopes of getting eight days leave for Xmas when I shall get one for you.

Remember me kindly to all old comrades, trusting all keep in the pink like.

Yours ever sincerely,
C. B. Jones

From 2nd Lieutenant J. Wilson   *1/7th West Yorkshire Regiment,*
BEF
12 December 1917

Dear Captain Weir,

Many thanks for your letter received here yesterday, also for your good wishes. Allow me to congratulate you as OC 'B' Coy, may the good luck continue. You will be pleased to hear that the 21st [OCB officers] are well represented in this unit, their names are Blackburn, Bell, Ingham, Chapman, Wheelton, 'A' Coy; Rogers, Panting, Nye & myself from 'B' Coy; and Jacques from 'D' Coy. Consequently I have a few friends. I gather from your letter that many changes have taken place at Crookham, my earnest wish is that they are for the better.

I was pleased you liked the photo, and think it was good. At present we are at Y[pres] and a pretty warm locum it is too. Fritz has a nasty habit of bombing us at night with his aircraft, and sometimes by day, which is not very pleasant, but is all in the day's work. Now I must ring off, with all good wishes to 'B' Co[mpany], more so No. 8 [Platoon].

I remain yours sincerely,
J. Wilson

From 2nd Lieutenant George P. Pick   *30 King's Avenue,*
Clapham Park, London
16 December 1917

Dear Captain Weir,

Although there is, as yet, very little to report, I think you may be interested to hear that I was able to see Colonel Luck at the Grosvenor Hotel this morning.

He is endeavouring to get an interview with AG 1 [part of the Adjutant-General's department] at the War Office on Monday morning, when I shall probably hear further. The Colonel apparently knows people on that branch of the Staff, so that the outlook is not too bad.

In fact I feel confident that I shall eventually get the decision[1] reversed, even if I do have to spend a few days at Sevenoaks.

May I take the opportunity of thanking you for the very useful advice and assistance you gave me.

Wherever I am I shall continue to follow the doings of 'B' [Company] and of No. 5 [Platoon], who, I hope, will soon make a sure thing of the platoon shield!

---

1. To deny Pick a commission in the British Army on account of his foreign-born parents.

> *Believe me to remain,*
> *Yours sincerely,*
> *George P. Pick*

From 2nd Lieutenant George P. Pick

30 King's Avenue,
Clapham Park, London
19 December 1917

Dear Captain Weir,

I am herewith enclosing a postal order for 3/1 in payment of photo which arrived today. I am very much obliged to you for having it forwarded.

In connexion with the other matter, there is little improvement to report: on Monday morning I accompanied Col[onel] Luck to a personal interview with a Major Wilson on the AG Staff at the WO [War Office]. The whole case was very carefully considered but they told us it was impossible to deviate in any way from an order that was recently laid down – namely that commissions would not be granted to anyone whose parents were not born in England.

Major Wilson added that they had had so many bad experiences with people coming under the category in question that they can make no exception in my case, remarkable though the circumstances were. Beyond this, he said there was absolutely nothing in the case. However I believe I shall obtain a transfer from the Middlesex Regt. & return to the Queen's, on Col. Luck's request.

I went to Sevenoaks yesterday, only to find the b[attalio]n had migrated to Reigate. So I returned to town and went to Reigate this morning, taking with me a letter from Col. Luck to the CO.

This, together with your own letter, already there, procured me ten days' leave on the spot, so I am now back in town again.

In spite of all the reverses, I am not without hope that something will eventually be done, although it may seem a little premature to speak about it.

It was splendid news to hear yesterday that Lt.-Col. A. D. Barton, DSO, commanding the 2/22 Londons (as successor to Col. Luck) had won the VC before Jerusalem & that the battalion had received inter alia three MCs & four MMs. Casualties are about 10%.

With very best wishes for Xmas and 1918 & many thanks for all you have done for me.

> *I remain,*
> *Yours sincerely,*
> *George P. Pick*

From 'Witters'   7th Royal West Kent Regiment, France
                                                      6 January 1918

My Dear old Natters,

*Just a line to wish you the proper thing for the New Year. As you will
see I really have arrived out here - got here a month ago in fact. I was
very lucky in getting my old job - signals - and am most comfortable bar
brief but painful periods.*

*I heard from Silkins a week ago - now a padre at Aldershot or some
such place.*

*Excuse more old thing - the best of luck. Let's have a line when you
get time.*

                                       Yours,
                                       Witters

From 2nd Lieutenant William Dobson   *17th King's Royal
                                                       Rifle Corps, BEF
                                                       14 January 1918*

Dear Sir,

*I am now taking the opportunity of writing you a few lines to say I
have landed with my battalion and company and settled down nicely.
Really it is a fine battalion, any amount of Scotch officers and I get on
with all of them - my Company Commander is Scotch also.*

*Have had one spell in the line so far and are at present resting. Of course
you know the usual working parties you get while on rest. How are all at
the OCB? I had a glimpse through the Incubator for November, but poor
old 'B' [Company] did not apparently get very far. I hope the next course
do. Neilson and nearly all 8 [Platoon] except White and McMillan came
out with me and have been posted to the various battalions. Of course
John Stewart still hangs it out at Sheerness. So far I haven't seen any
names in the casualty list yet. I had a letter from Richardson, 6 Platoon,
who has landed in Italy with the 18th Battalion. Now this is all meantime
as am Orderly Officer. Trusting you are well.*

Cheero.

                                       Yours truly,
                                       William Dobson

Top: Grandson Michael Weir Burns retraces Neil Weir's footsteps over 95 years later. Longueval and Delville wood can be seen on the horizon.

Above: Mike Burns holding a copy of the original map standing on the very spot where his grandfather set up a command post.

Above right: Mike Burns finds the grave of one of Weir's comrades.

Right: Reflecting on how many lives were lost, in Delville Wood cemetery.

11-10-16

My Dear Mother

Just a line to say
I was wounded by
a rocket light
yesterday. My
leg is burnt from
the knee up to
the thigh —
Go down to the
Base to-day, but

I don't expect it is
bad enough to get
to Blighty with
Perhaps it is all
for the best as
we were just going
to have for ships
"Go"
I will let you
know my new
address,

Yor Reid

Mrs Reid
Lower Broadheath
Worcester
England

POST OFFICE TELEGRAPHS.

TO Mrs Reid the Cottage
Lower Broadheath nr Worcester

... Reid ... Sutherland Highlanders admitted
13 Genl Hospital Rouen
with burn right thigh
Secy War office

FIELD SERVICE POST CARD

A.F.A. 2042.
114. Gen. No. 5240.

The address
only to be writ-
ten on this side.
If anything else
is added, the
post card will
be destroyed.

(Crown Copyright Reserved)

Mrs Reid Broadheath
Lower Worcester
England

NOTHING is to be written on this side except
the date and signature of the sender. Sentences
not required may be erased. If anything else is
added the post card will be destroyed.

I am quite well.
I have been admitted into hospital
{ sick } and am going on well.
{ wounded } and hope to be discharged soon.
I am being sent down to the base.
I have received your { letter dated
{ telegram
{ parcel
Letter follows at first opportunity
I have received no letter from you
{ lately.
{ for a long time.

Signature
only. Reid A. Reid

Date 11-9-16

[Postage must be prepaid on any letter or post card
addressed to the sender of this card.]

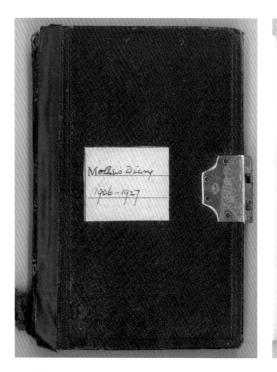

Opposite page: Weir's letter (*top*) from the Somme to his mother informing her of his injury, 11 October 1916; its envelope (*centre left*); Mrs Weir's official telegram of 15 October (*centre right*); and the Field Service Post Card (*bottom, both*) Weir was able to send to his mother on the 12th.

Above: Dorothy Weir's diary, covering twenty-one years, has been kept with her son's papers. Each page is beautifully written. This section describes her first visit to Neil whilst he was in hospital recovering from his injury.

OFFICERS OF Nos. 20 AND 21 OFFICER CADET PATTALIONS.

——CROOKHAM, HANTS, MARCH, 1918.——

Gale & Polden Ltd.
ALDERSHOT

Back Row—Lt. N. W. Hazser   Capt. J. N. Muir   Lt. G. B. Mackie   Lt. M. Gordon   Lt. R. L. Paton   Capt. G. Anderton   Capt. J. H. Suarue   Lt. J. P. Day, A.C.   Capt. D. Atenhead   Lt. J. C. F. Newman   Capt. S. E. Baker

Fourth Row—Capt. C. S. Fuller   Capt. N. Syddall, R.E.   Capt. G. Gregson-Ellis, M.C.   Capt. J. Bennett   Capt. W. J. C. Fleming   Capt. A. F. Mills, M.C.   Capt. D. Addison, M.C.   Capt. R. C. E. Holmes   Capt. C. Wallis

Contd.—Capt. J. R. Worthinston   Lt. W. F. I. Oliver, M.C.   Capt. J. P. Wild   Lt. J. P. Pither   Capt. L. A. Elsworth

Third Row—Lt. R. G. J. Booth   Capt. G. J. Colimer, M.C.   Capt. L. E. Judkins   Lt. J. MacTaggart   Lt. & Qrmr. A. W. Cole   Capt. F. C. Stigant   Capt. G. S Beale   Capt. A. Mc. K. Forsyth, M.C.   Capt. R. W. Chetham-Strode, M.C.

Contd.—Lt. R. Edridge, R.A.M.C.   Capt. R. A. Amtier   Capt. C. M. Wright, M.C., M.M.

Second Row—Capt. H. J. Diamond   Lt. & Qrmr. H. R. Harrison   Capt. A. T. Hunt   Capt. The Hon. L. Lindsay, M.C.   Capt. F. H. R. Maunsell   Capt. N. A. C. Weir   Capt. C. A. E. Chudleigh   Major A. L. Ashwell, D.S.O.   Capt. F. C. Baldwyn

Contd.—Capt. R. W. Nicholson   Capt. J. B. Coates   Capt. R. L. Bradley   Capt. E. W. Shann   Capt. D. MacLeod

Front Row—Major A. Whittle   Major J. N. Wadmore   Major S. J. M. Sampson, M.C.   Capt. & Adjt. J. S. Gaskell   Major H. St. J. Jefferies, D.S.O.   Lt.-Col. A. V. Usater, C.M.G.   Lt.-Col. H. W. Smith, D.S.O.   Major P. S. Wates

Contd.—Capt. & Adjt. E. B. Mulliner   Major O. B. Haines   Major E. W. Mayhew, M.C.   Major S. B. Skevinston

21st O.C.B. "B" COMPANY. No. 7 PLATOON. MAY, 1917.

"B" COMPANY HOCKEY XI.

February, 1918.

Left: Captain N. A. C. Weir, with fellow officers of 20th and 21st OCBs. Weir is in the 2nd row up, 6th from the left, wearing his Highlanders' glengarry.

Top: Weir, in uniform, with his officer cadets.

Above: Weir (middle row, 2nd from left) still wearing a bandage covering the leg wound he received 15 months earlier.

Above: Neil Archibald Campbell Weir's birth certificate, 25 April 1895.

Right: His letter of appointment to the 10th Argylls, 27 August 1914, at the age of 19.

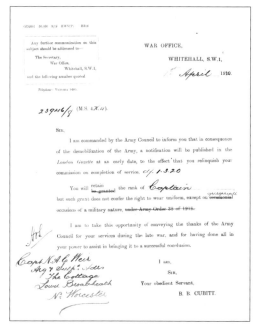

Weir's notice of demobilization, dated as 1 April 1920, in fact after his service ended.

Weir's official demobilization certificate, 1 March 1920.

Above, both: Captain Neil Archibald Campbell Weir, OBE, MBE, CMG, Argyll and Sutherland Highlanders.

The young 2nd Lieutenant Weir with the motorbike he bought in 1914.

Captain Weir of the Colonial Service.

This is to Certify that
Capt. N. A. C. Weir.
10th Arg. & Suth. Highrs.
is a Member of the Ypres
League of Officers and
Men who served in the
Immortal Defence of Ypres
1914-1918

The War of 1914-1918.

Argyll & Sutherland Highlanders
T/Capt. N. A. C. Weir, 10th Bn.

was mentioned in a Despatch from

General Sir Douglas Haig, G.C.B., K.C.I.E., K.C.V.O., A.D.C.

dated 13th November 1916

for gallant and distinguished services in the Field.

I have it in command from the King to record His Majesty's

high appreciation of the services rendered.

Winston S. Churchill

War Office
Whitehall, S.W.
1st March 1919.

Secretary of State for War.

War Diary   February–April 1918

In the middle of February [1918] the course was increased by the War Office [from five] to six months and so it was decided that 'A' & 'B' Companies should pass out 50% at the end of that month. My 50% over and 'A' Company's would stay on for an extra month under my supervision and that of my officers. This was a horrid arrangement but couldn't be helped and the 'A' Company fellows took the whole extra month to get into our ways. Meanwhile Colonel Smith was sick and Usher and Muir left. Phillips of the York and Lancs took Muir's place.

This last month was amusing. I let the cadets run their own show and we spent our time in attending demonstrations etc. We visited the various Aldershot Command schools and I think this method was a success. However this ended on March 31st.

I didn't think I should return but I was ordered back to start the 4th course, a real good lot of fellows and I was sorry to hand over to Shevington of 'E' Company. He belonged to the London Irish. And so I left at the end of April.

This life was a great experience and as I look back I am thankful that I was given the opportunity of passing through it, thanks to Hardy.

From **M. A. McGregor**[1]   *20 Clarendon Place, Stirling*
                                                        3 April 1918

Dear Capt[ain] Weir,

It is most generous of you to send us such a large cheque for the Prisoners of War Fund of the A & S Highlanders. Colonel Tweedie forwarded it on this morning. We are all very grateful & I write to send the warmest thanks of the Committee. We are having such splendid support from the Officers & Men of the A & S Highlanders just now it is most encouraging.

                            Sincerely yours,
                            M. A. McGregor

From **2nd Lieutenant C. B. Wilson**   *28 Addington Road, Reading*
                                                        9 April 1918

Dear Weir,

Thanks so much for your letter, it took rather a long time to get here as it went home first. As you will see [from the RAF letter heading] I have

---

1. Vice-President of the Argyll & Sutherland Highlanders Prisoners of War Fund.

at last managed to persuade the Air Force[1] that I am really quite fit. I had to have an operation on my nose before I could manage it. I have been here about a month & have another fortnight to go, after that three weeks leave & then I go to a squadron. What is Crookham like without Col. Dickson? It can't be quite the same place with all due respect to the present CO. That doesn't sound very nice does it but you know what I mean don't you? All the men who were posted to the LFs with me went out [to France] when I went to hospital before Christmas. I mean Alex Wilson, L. A. Wilson, and one or two of the 21st men. R. G. has been through this school & is now at a squadron & I'm doing my best to get the 'wings up' [become a qualified pilot] before he does. My younger brother is here on the same course so there will be three Wilsons flying. Do you still use your motor bike & do you ever come near Reading? If you do will you come here & have tea with us some day? By the way, talking of motor bikes, I have never forgiven myself for breaking your piston ring. I should like to put another on for you just to show you that I can do it.

I met Urinuski (I can't spell it) here on the observer's course & he had met heaps of the old 'D' Co[mpan]y over there. He also said he ran into Major Finch at a Command School – still lecturing on outposts.

It is awfully good of you to tell me all about the 21st as it is all so interesting. I only wish the course had been six months when I was there.

Thanks very much, my wife is very fit & wishes to be remembered to you.

> *Yours truly,*
> *C. Bernard Wilson*

From Jonathan Knowling

North Bay House,
Tenby, South Wales
10 April 1918

Dear Captain Weir,
I know you will forgive my delay in answering your very kind letter. I have heard so much of you from Jack [known to his fellow officers as Dick], from the very beginning when he sent us proofs of the Regiment. It is difficult to realize that his soldier days are over; he was so keen on the work, but still as he was originally intended for the army one must remember that his death in action is a fitting end to his career. He was so delighted on being able to get back to his old regiment & wrote very cheerily to the end. It's a great comfort to me to feel that he was

---

1. On 1 April 1918 the Royal Naval Air Service (RNAS) merged with the Army's Royal Flying Corps (RFC) to form the Royal Air Force, the third service.

beloved by his brother officers from whom I have received so many avid expressions of respect & sympathy. Please accept my very grateful thanks for your kind letter.

Yours sincerely,
Jonathan Knowling

From Captain N. McQueen

In the Field
14 April 1918

My Dear Weir,

Many thanks for your letter. I was v. sorry not to see you at home but the fates were agin it. I have given your congrats to Peter [Bonnyman]. He is still here but far from well. He has also collected an MC. He is a great soldier & has done most awfully well.

We are in another Div[ision] as you probably know. It is rather a blow. The diced hosetops & glengarries have arrived & the Band have specially asked me as Band President to convey their thanks & great appreciation of your kindness – it was very good of you. Very many thanks.

The CO keeps wonderfully fit & cheery & sends his best love & says don't be a B.F. [bloody fool] & come out again.

Tubby Nial has left us & is now Camp Commandant to a Corps.

The weather does not help, it is damned cold. But we are keeping v. cheery.

From
McQueen

11.

Reserve Battalion

—————

Weir left the 21st Officer Cadet Battalion at the end of April 1918 in the firm belief that he was about to be sent back to France. Instead, to his intense disappointment, he was posted to the 3rd (Reserve) Battalion, Argyll & Sutherland Highlanders, which was stationed in Ireland and used as a training and feeder unit for the battalions on active service. His first month-long stint in County Cork coincided with a brief hiatus between the second and third (of five) German offensives on the Western Front.

From the start of the war, most volunteers had joined their local infantry reserve battalions for training. But after the introduction of conscription in January 1916, the existing regimental structure could no longer cope with the rush of new recruits and a centralized training and reserve system was introduced. In September 1916, as part of this centralization, regimental affiliations were discontinued and the reserve battalions renumbered from 1 to 116. But the detrimental effect this had on regimental esprit de corps was acknowledged in May 1917 when the reserve battalions were reaffiliated with particular regiments. Weir was fortunate enough to join the reserve system after this error had been reversed. Yet his diary confirms that the system was still far from perfect, with most officers regarding reserve duty as an opportunity to 'have a good slack' and take 'little or no interest in the Battalion or his military duties'. He was more than thankful when, after just one month with the 3rd Argylls, he was given the chance to train as a staff officer.

War Diary   April–May 1918

After leaving the 21st Officer Cadet Battalion at the end of April 1918, I received rather a shock. Instead of getting my orders for France, which I was expecting, I was ordered to join my Reserve Battalion, the 3rd Argyll and Sutherland Highlanders, who were stationed at Charles Fort, Kinsale, County Cork, Ireland.

This was unpleasant as the 3rd Battalion is not a place where one can work. After a rotten journey via Holyhead and Dublin, I duly arrived at Cork only to find that Kinsale Camp was out of bounds owing to an outbreak of measles.

For the time, therefore, I was attached to the 3rd King's Regiment in Victoria Barracks and there was a detachment of Argylls there consisting of about 12 officers and 200 men.

At the end of a fortnight, we received orders to move down to Kinsale, a distance of 22-odd miles by train with a change at Kinsale Junction.

On arriving there I found that part of the Battalion were accommodated in Charles Fort and part in Forthill camp. The officers, for the most part were in Charles Fort but the Mess was in Forthill Camp. As a matter of fact, those stationed in the Fort did not draw field allowance, while those in the camp did, so the Colonel had decreed that the senior officers should live in the Fort, while subalterns lived in the camp and therefore a subaltern was getting as much pay as a captain.

The Commanding Officer was Brevet Colonel J. Wolrige Gordon, CMG, late of the 93rd.

The second-in-command was Major Maxwell-Rouse a Special Reservist and the Adjutant was Captain J. Neill, MC, a regular who had had the misfortune to lose an arm early in the war. Almost at once, I was appointed OC 'B' Company, a company of recruits. At the same time the Colonel asked me to take over the Young Officers' Company from Captain Muirhead, MC.

From a Company Commander's point of view, I had nothing to do except take the Company Orderly Room and attend the Commanding Officer's Orderly Room, if I had a prisoner.

The other great event of the week was the Saturday morning barrack inspection and a Thursday kit inspection. Otherwise one never saw one's company for the rest of the week as they were all at different stages of training, which was run by the Adjutant.

By the way I must not forget the Friday route march – one of the best things in the week – which everyone was supposed to attend. On this occasion one heard the brass band, an exceptionally good band and the pipe band also assisted.

Needless to say it was not the last word in route marching, but the Colonel tried to set a good example by marching himself. The Young Officers' Company kept me busy. Everyone knows the attitude the officer of a Reserve Battalion takes up. He thinks he is there to have a good slack and he takes little or no interest in the Battalion or his military duties. Regular, Special Reservist or Temporary – they are all alike.

Although I do not hold with Young Officer squads there is one thing to be said for them and that is they keep the fellow employed. A reserve battalion is a bad place for every type of officer, but it is a fearful place for the newly gazetted officer who has been through a hard training at Sandhurst or a cadet battalion.

These fellows did not prove the exception and I had a very hard time to get them all together as a class. If a fellow did not attend he always had some excuse and while I was taking a class, my assistant, Lieutenant Gordon Patterson, spent his time in routing them out of bed etc.

There were no facilities for training and when one conducted a tactical tour, one generally ended up in a field out of bounds to the military. I cannot say more of the classes. We ran them as best we could. I certainly was the best hated officer in the Mess.

Boating and sailing were the chief forms of recreation at Kinsale. Football had to be played on the parade ground. Fortunately there was a good gymnasium in the camp, which could be used in wet weather. The Mess was well conducted and Tuesday was adopted as Guest night. The Colonel was very particular about dinner every evening.

Luckily for my sake I was ordered by the War Office to proceed on a Staff Learner's Course[1] at the end of May, so I ended my first period with my Reserve Battalion at the end of a short month there.

From Captain W. S. Stevenson

Divisional Staff, In the Field
Monday 29 April 1918

Dear Weary,

I'm afraid I'm a frightfully bad correspondent so far as you are concerned. I've just got the letter you sent to Muswell Hill and I'm sorry you've had such bad luck with all your good intentions.

This is the 29th, the day you are joining the 3rd Battalion and I hope you don't find Ireland a most distasteful country. I should think you wouldn't be long with the 3rd Battalion if you have been [graded as fit for] GS so long and I hope to see you in France again, though it is too much to hope that you will come to us.

Just heard that French, who is second-in-command of the BW, has been given a bar to his MC.

Ned MacMillan is still here with the Brigade helping the Staff Captain. He had rather a shaking the other day when the Staff Captain was killed practically by his side and has gone off to Le Touquet to recuperate for a week. Ronald Cavendish could only have been wounded slightly and at duty for I heard from McQueen about the same day as the report appeared and he said Rosie [Cavendish] was still with the Battalion.

---

1. A Staff Learner was a junior staff position in the Quartermaster (Logistics) Branch of a Brigade Headquarters. He was usually a captain or a lieutenant, and junior to the unit's General Staff Officer 3.

Bill Lumsden turned up the other day. His battalion is now back here minus Maxwell Forsythe, who died of wounds received during a raid.

I am still with the [9th] Division, I am glad to say. Extraordinary luck I have had in staying with them though I have changed jobs twice since you left.

I'm blowed if I can tell you how to get to France unless you simply get on the boat and come out. Your CO with the Reserve Battalion ought to be able to send you out fairly soon this time.

Let me know when you have any luck.

Ever yours,
Staggers

From 2nd Lieutenant J. Wilson

In Flanders
19 May 1918

Dear Captain Weir,

I have just received my Incubator for Feb. In it I noticed my old platoon had again lifted the shield. My best wishes to yourself & the victorious platoon. From this I gather they are keeping up the reputation in great style, may the success continue. I am very fit and well just now, and at the time of writing I am engaged as a drill instructor at a school for junior NCOs. We had the Div[isiona]l Commander down to see us the other day, and at the close he congratulated me on the excellent show we made. He described it as devilish good. My address is attached 146 Inf[antry] B[riga]de School. All the Crookham boys are quite fit except Parker, late of No. 7, who is in the hos[pital] with a bruised ankle. Soon I hope to be sweating on the top line for leave. Now I will dry up writing. Yourself, the Company you have the honour to command, and No 8 Platoon, the best of luck.

I remain your very sincerely,
J. Wilson, 2nd/Lt
1/7 W. Yorks

From Captain N. McQueen

In the Field
24 May 1918

My Dear Weir,

Ever so many thanks for the silver inscription plate for the pipers of 'B' – I have handed it to Thomson who is commanding & you will no doubt hear from him.

The Colonel is very keen to know what YOC[1] stands for. Is it a young officer's class or a Sinn Fein organization?

When are you coming out again? We shall be delighted to see you again.

We have seen John D[ashwood] several times lately. He is at the moment living with the next B[attalio]n HQ. He looks ever so much more fit & is full of beans.

Is Sergeant Simpson (Tubby) of 'C' Co[mpan]y with the 3rd? I am very keen to get him back if he is.

My respects to the Colonel & Rouse.

From
McQueen

---

1. It stood for Young Officers' Company, 3rd Argylls.

12.

Staff Learner

——◦∞◦——

During the three months that Weir spent as a trainee staff officer in England, from June to late August 1918, the BEF's war on the Western Front took a decisive turn for the better.

At first the omens were not good as the third German offensive ('Blucher') against the British and French in Champagne (27 May–4 June) took the Allied defenders by surprise. The Germans advanced 13 miles on the first day, and a further 17 by the end of the third. By 3 June they were just 56 road miles from Paris, having taken 50,000 prisoners and severed the main railway line from Paris to Nancy. On 5 June, the British Cabinet discussed evacuating the BEF. Up to a million people fled from Paris. Yet the situation was stabilized by American troops and reserves moved by Foch from Flanders.[1]

A fourth attack ('Gneisenau') was made from this new salient on 9 June, but it was anticipated and beaten back. Pétain halted the counter-offensive on 15 June to conserve men. One final offensive was launched over the Marne on 15 July by 52 German divisions; but the Allies, including US troops, counter-attacked in strength and by 4 August had captured 30,000 prisoners and 600 guns, at a cost of 160,000 casualties to the Germans' 110,000.[2]

During these five offensives the Germans captured ten times more territory than the Allies had done in 1917, and extended the line of the Western Front by 75 miles. But their casualties were nearly a million, men they could not replace. The Allies, on the other hand, could count on American reinforcements. From May to October, over 200,000 Americans disembarked in France every month, with their total numbers rising from 284,000 at the end of March to almost 1.9 million by the start of November. Ludendorff's gamble had failed and now it was the Allies' turn.[3]

On 24 July, after a meeting with Haig, Pétain and Pershing (the US commander), Foch circulated a memorandum (largely the work of his chief of staff, Maxime Weygand) that said the Allies had reached the 'turning point': now they had the advantage and would keep it by a rapid sequence of

1. Stevenson, *1914–1918*, pp. 417–18.
2. Ibid., pp. 423–4.
3. Ibid., p. 420.

limited blows to clear the transverse railways running eastwards from Paris towards Avricourt and north towards Amiens, as well as pinching out the St-Mihiel salient in Lorraine; other operations might push the Germans back from the Channel ports and advance towards the Saar coalfield. In other words they would deliver sharp surprise attacks aimed at concrete objectives, and suspend them before the enemy fed in reserves and casualties mounted. Foch did not expect victory until 1919.[1]

Haig had already submitted proposals for what became the Battle of Amiens (8–12 August) to be commanded by Rawlinson of the Fourth Army. It was to be a spectacular massed tank operation, using 552 vehicles that included Mark Vs and the new lighter Whippet tanks (capable of up to 8mph) and armoured cars. With a local superiority of four to one in air-craft (many German planes were still in Champagne), the British and French could prevent overflights and ensure surprise, as well as support the ground advance. But artillery had also developed, and while the heavy guns silenced the enemy batteries with phosgene gas and high explosive, the field guns shielded the infantry with a creeping barrage.

The attack by 50,000 men began at 4:20 a.m. on 8 August, without a pre-liminary bombardment, across dry ground and under cover of mist. By mid-afternoon the Allies had advanced up to eight miles, suffering losses of 9,000 but inflicting three times that number on their enemies, and capturing 12,000 prisoners and over 400 guns. Even beyond the creeping barrage the attackers could still move forward, suppressing machine guns with tanks, although most of the latter broke down or were hit by artillery as the day wore on.[2]

The role played in the battle by the 10th Argylls was related to Weir in a letter from Quartermaster-Sergeant Brodie of 'B' Company, dated 19 August. It contained the sad news that Captain Bonnyman, one of only two original officers still with the 10th, was killed in the attack. A quite separate source, Wing Commander Archibald James of the RAF, recorded in his memoirs a chance meeting with Colonel Sotheby, his adjutant and a runner in a field close to the front line on the second day of the offensive. 'At this point,' recalled James,

> a German sniper intervened and started shooting at us long range
> – somewhere about 700 yards. The trio was so exhausted that they
> paid not the slightest attention to the bullets, which came unpleasantly
> close; I had to insist that we take cover in a shell hole, while I finished
> my notes. I asked the Colonel to give me the coordinates of the flanks
> of his battalion . . . He gave me the position and I queried it . . . Further
> cross-examination solved the confusion. His division had been de-

---

1. Stevenson, *1914–1918*, pp. 424–5.
2. Ibid., p. 426.

trained in the dark and had marched up through the night; from the very outset they had mistaken their position in this slightly rolling countryside where the typical villages, such as those nearest us ... look surprisingly alike. Under this delusion the Colonel had imagined himself to be more than a mile to the north of his real position. Our meeting illustrated not only the danger of topographical confusion but also the more direct danger that was the cause of many deaths; the anaesthesia of fatigue.[1]

That same day, 9 August, the Canadians advanced another four miles, though they had fewer tanks and the heavy guns could not be moved up to provide effective counter-battery fire. On 11 August Rawlinson, aware of the mounting difficulties, called a halt to the attack. Final British and French casualties were each around 22,000; the Germans lost 75,000 (including 50,000 POWs).[2]

The significance of the battle is that it severely shook the confidence of the German High Command. On 13 August, Ludendorff told Hindenburg, his co-commander, that the only course now was a defensive strategy with occasional limited attacks in the hope of wearing down the Allies and forcing them to come to terms.[3]

War Diary   June 1918

I was ordered to report at the Headquarters of the 208th Infantry Brigade, who were stationed at Welbeck Camp, near Worksop, Nottinghamshire, on the 1st June, 1918. This was my preliminary canter in the Learner's course. I arrived at Worksop Station late in the evening, only to find that the Camp was some 3 miles distant. Taxis to the rescue!

The camp was situated quite near the stables at Welbeck Abbey in grounds belonging to the Duke of Portland. The Brigade Headquarters were actually in the stables, which was about a quarter of a mile distant from the house itself. The Brigade Officers' Mess consisted of a small marquee in the camp and the officers attached to the Brigade Staff lived in bell tents close by. Other units of the brigade were in lines near by. This was the first time I had been under canvas during the war but luckily the weather was fine with only an occasional thunderstorm. The senior officer in the Brigade Mess was the Brigade Musketry Officer, Captain W. J. Shaw, MC, Rifle Brigade. The General lived out, as did the Staff Captain. The Brigade-Major was away on the Staff Course at Cambridge.

---

1. An extract from the unpublished memoirs of Sir Archibald James, MP, Private Collection.
2. Stevenson, *1914–1918*, p. 427.
3. Ibid.

The Learner's duties at the Brigade consisted of understudying the Staff Captain for ten days and then understudying the Brigade-Major for ten days. As a matter of fact this was not so in our case, owing to the fact that the Brigade-Major was away.

The other Learner, Captain C. L. T. Matheson, MC, RE, and myself spent all our time in the Staff Captain's office.

We used to take one day indoors and one day out. The latter was naturally the more pleasant of the two as we spent our time riding about, inspecting the camp, etc.

Luckily the weather kept fine and so we had plenty of tennis on the courts at Welbeck and even if it rained we got a game on the hard court in the riding school there. The Brigade also held sports, a swimming gala and a horse show. Concerts were also given to the men at Welbeck Abbey.

After twenty-one days we both left with a recommendation from the General.

208th Infantry Brigade

Brigade Commander	Brigadier-General F. F. W. Daniell
Brigade-Major	Major R. H. Waithman, DSO, R. Sussex Regt.
Staff Captain	Captain T. A. MacArthur, Cheshire Regt.
Orderly Officer	Lieutenant E. B. N. Butterworth, York & Lancs
Musketry Officer	Captain W. J. Shaw, MC
51st Graduated Battalion, KOYLI	
	Lieutenant-Colonel F. A. Wilson
51st Graduated Battalion, Notts & Derby Regt.	
	Lieutenant-Colonel J. H. Collett, CMG
52nd Graduated Battalion, KOYLI	
	Lieutenant-Colonel A. J. Ellis, DSO
52nd Notts & Derby Regt.	Lieutenant-Colonel C. G. Lambton, DSO

Before I leave Welbeck, I should like to mention what a lovely place it was. The grounds and park were beautiful and of course I should mention the famous underground passages.[1]

---

1. A previous owner of Welbeck Abbey, the eccentric 5th Duke of Portland (1800–79), had had constructed under the building a maze of underground rooms and tunnels that are said to have run for 15 miles. The subterranean chambers – all of which were painted pink – included a great hall (160 feet long), a library (250 feet), an observatory with a glass roof and a vast billiards room.

From **Captain W. S. Stevenson**   *In the Field*
                                                  Monday 10 June 1918

Dear Weary,

Many thanks for your letter. Ned MacMillan blew in here almost simultaneously with it and when I showed him the envelope, remarked the one word 'NACKERS!' MacMillan has just returned from leave and goes off to join the Battalion [10th Argylls] tomorrow.

I heard from McQueen the other day. They have made Woodburn a major which I believe ought to make us substantive majors pari passu as the book says, but I am getting further particulars and will let you have them when they arrive or when I see it in the [London] Gazette!

Cavendish has left them now and is a GSO 3. Third Army I believe. Young Rait is now pukka Staff Captain and achieved an MC in the last Gazette. General Kennedy is at the moment on leave, due back about the 23rd.

Hope your course will develop into something in the near future, either a job out here or a month or two's good value to Cambridge, which of course you despise as a centre of learning.

Bertie Bankier of the 93rd is now BM 26[th Brigade] so they are all of the tribe. Bill Lumsden suddenly found himself with two DSOs the other day to his great astonishment and everyone's delight. Joe Scott is DAAG [Deputy Assistant Adjutant-General] in this Corps, so we rather swarm round here, in spite of the lamentable exodus of the Battalion [to 32nd Division] which I haven't got over yet. Let me have some more news of you.

Staggers

War Diary   June–August 1918

30 June 1918: After leaving Welbeck at the end of twenty-one days, I was ordered to report to Officer Commanding 348th Artillery Brigade, Royal Field Artillery, which was stationed at Carburton Camp about 3.5 miles from Welbeck and 4 miles from Worksop. The Brigade, which consisted of four batteries, lived in the same camp as the 69th Divisional Ammunition Column under the command of Lieutenant-Colonel M. M. Duncan, CMG, and Lieutenant-Colonel R. D. Wylde respectively. All the officers of the Brigade messed together.

It was decided that I should be attached to 'C' Battery (Major Ferguson in command). The other two Learners, Middleton and Attoe, were attached to 'B' & 'D' Batteries.

The seventeen-odd days I spent with the battery were extremely interesting. First of all I was taught Gun Drill, Laying etc. and after went out with the Battery for field work. When we paraded on these days we did not return to lunch but stayed out the whole day. The weather kept fine.

During the weekends I managed to get over to Welbeck for tennis. Four days in this office was quite long enough to get some faint idea of the working of a headquarters office.

Attoe and I were ordered to report to Divisional Headquarters the same day and were lucky enough to get a divisional car to take us over from Carburton to Retford.

69th Divisional Artillery

CRA	Brigadier-General L. A. C. Gordon, CB, CSI
Brigade-Major	Major A. E. Newland, DSO, RA
Staff Captain	Major W. Moore, RA
ADC	Lieut E. Fitz McLean, RA
Attached	Captain Healy, RFA

348th Artillery Brigade

OC	Lieut.-Col. M. M. Duncan, CMG
Adjutant	Captain P. W. Devitt, MC
'A' Battery	—
'B' Battery	Major Ubsdell, DSO
'C' Battery	Acting Major Ferguson
'D' Battery	Captain Ashton

69th Divisional DAC

OC	Lieut-Col R. D. Wylde

19 July 1918: My next duty was to report at the Headquarters of the 69th Division for a tour of instruction at the Divisional Headquarters for six weeks. The Headquarters were actually situated in West Retford House, quite one of the largest houses in the town. Retford itself is an uninteresting town of the manufacturing variety and possessing a mayor and corporation with one large parish church and one good hotel, the White Hart.

Attoe and I had decided to get digs together and in this we had some difficulty as all the feasible places were occupied by Staff or RAF cadets, who seemed to abound. However we were lucky enough to get a decent bedroom and sitting room in the Albany Hotel, a temperance place.

To get back to our duties. First of all, I was attached to the 'A' side for ten days under the DAAG, Major R. J. K. Mott, MC. After this I came under the DAQMG, Major Moore, who went off on leave after I had been with him for five days and so I was left to carry on with those duties. I enjoyed this, although I had no more idea of the duties of a 'Q' man than the 'man in the moon'. However Lieutenant-Colonel A. W. Wallace, the AA&QMG kept a strict eye on me.

From Captain W. S. Stevenson   *3 August 1918*

Dear N. A. C. Weir,

Thank you so much for your encouraging letter – as it happens I am quite well.

I found the battalion had floated up north recently, so I went over to call on them with young Rait. Saw Sotheby just back from leave at Deauville, also Bonnyman, McQueen, Woodburn and lots of the old men I used to know. Only three of my platoon now remaining: one with transport, one with the man ['old man'?, i.e commanding officer], and one as HQ sanitary man – what a fall for No. 16, once the brightest and best of the platoons!

Woodburn is a major vice French, dated 19th November 1917, and I have put in to be a pukka major on the strength of this. I can't see why the same thing doesn't apply to you but I'm not up on home rulings. The 'A' fellow [Administrative staff officer] in your office ought to be able to tell you all about it – in fact you ought to know all about it yourself if you are an efficient creeper [slang for staff officer] as I am sure you must be.

Ned [MacMillan] hasn't got a job yet. He's still creeping with the new Brigade in the 32nd Division. He also attended the dinner party the other night. [Brigadier-]General [J.] Kennedy [former CO of the 10th Argylls] has just gone home on six month's tour of duty. You ought to try to get into touch with him at the Cale[donian] Club or elsewhere, as I'm sure he'll welcome you with open arms if he happens to have a vacancy at any time with his home Brigade. Don't quite know where he's going as he's having a fortnight's leave first.

French did very well the other day in the METEREN show – you may have read a little about it.[1]

Buzzing off to lunch now.

> *Au revoir.*
> *W. S.*

---

1. Stevenson was referring to the leading role that French and his battalion of the Black Watch (part of the 9th Division) had played both in the capture of Méteren in Flanders on 19 July, and in the repulse of a German counter-attack a week later.

From **Quartermaster-Sergeant J. Brodie**   *In the Field*
                                                      3 August 1918

Dear Sir,

*I take the pleasure of writing a few lines to you hoping you are in the
pink and prospering. Some men of the recent drafts were telling me you
were in Kinsale. A few of the drafts have been posted to 'B' Coy from
your 'B' Coy at Kinsale. And of course they were asked about you, as you
are not forgotten in the Coy. You have the distinction of being longest
in command of 'B' Coy. I think since you left we hold the record for Coy
officers. Probably you would like to know the verdict of the men from your
Coy [who] have joined your late Coy. Well it is the same as they thought
about you when you were here. We are at present having a rest after a
long spell in the line (rest from the trenches only) near a place you are
pretty familiar with. You remember where you used to come staggering
into in the dark & mud looking for the QMS [Quartermaster-Sergeant, i.e.
Brodie] to get settled in your huts. We are all feeling bucked up again &
expect to be having a hot time shortly. The Coy is in a remarkably good
condition at present having fallen victims to the polishing craze, being
quite up to date with service chevrons, wound bars and refitting. You
will probably remember L/Cpl Spencer. I was talking to him. He told me
you considered he was likely to get promotion when he came out here.
All the old hands in the Coy (Sgt. Lyle is back) join in thanking you for
your thoughtfulness in asking often of them and in return send their
best regards to you. I am sorry to say Sgt. Haggerty was wounded and
died of his wounds the following day, also Sgt. Hamilton died of wounds
a short time back. The only original officers in the Batt[alion] are Major
McQueen and Captain Bonnyman. We could be doing with a few more of
them, with all due respect to the others.*

*I wonder who your CSM and QMS are at Kinsale. If I knew [who] I
would know what like a Coy it is. Captain Ramsay is in command of
'B' Company. He has been awarded an MC for a recent bombing stunt
in which 'B' Company took part, covered by 'D' Company. It was very
successful, the object being gained and prisoners taken back with the loss
of 1 man wounded (not badly), 40030 Private Duncan. I think you will
know him. I will have to close for want of news. Hoping this finds you in
the very best of health and prospering.*

                              Yours sincerely,
                              J. Brodie

From Quartermaster-Sergeant J. Brodie

Dear Sir,

Thanks for letter. This is a quick return to yours seeing I have a little time to spare and have just taken your note from my pocket, so will try and let you know a little of the strenuous time we have had since you wrote till now. We were having a rest and had just had a visit from His Majesty [King George V]: you speak about [causing a] stir, well he walked through the camp (at Ypres). We got a hurried order to move, rather unexpected as we thought we were to take part in the do there. Entrained, embussed and marched with short rests until we took an objective, doing our part in the advance, passing through Amiens in busses to the vicinity of an old post which we had already twice visited before on the same errand. After our part had been done we have been marched back & had a couple of nights sleep in the open on retaken ground and are now in another sector. Pretty quiet considering the Boche have lately flitted. I think we will likely have another trip over the sticks as we have not suffered nearly as much as some other regiments, being rather lucky as regards the amount of casualties. But very unlucky to lose some of the very best. Captain Bonnyman got killed, one of the original 10th officers & I suppose you will have heard about it. 'C' Company lost company officers, SM & QMS killed. 'B' Company had no casualties to officers, although we did not get off too lightly. Andrews took over 'C' Company. We are going through the usual process of getting drafts, re-organising, refitting etc. Still the news keeps good which helps to lighten things. Hoping this finds you in the very best of health and prospering.

Yours,
J. Brodie

From 2nd Lieutenant K. A. Angin

My Dear Weir,

Very many apologies for not having answered your letter before but life has been very full recently & little time to myself.

Yes, I've joined the flying [Corps], not exactly out of choice because life here, except when I arrive home, is the worst experience of soldiering I've ever had I think. The place is badly run, there is no discipline & the vast majority of officers openly boast that they only wanted six months more home service (!) & are not keen on the job. However, there is one fellow

of my battalion & several others I know so it might be worse. There are
many ex-cadets of 'B' Co[mpan]y here.

I heard from Muir[1] a day or so ago: he is at an Army School with
[Captain] Jones & has been very lucky in recent fighting apparently.

I'm very keen on this new job here flying, as you know I was & the
work here I find vastly interesting but the majority of the instructors are
extremely poor although there are notable exceptions.

I wish you luck in your job and hope the regular commission will be
all right. My wife wishes to be remembered to you.

> *Yours,*
> *K. A. Angin*

War Diary　August 1918

After a fortnight with 'Q', I was attached to the General Staff Officer 3 and
Attoe was at that time acting in this capacity, as Hart-Davis was away on
a course.

This was quite an exciting time as the [69th] Division were constantly
receiving orders for emergency moves etc., and General Robertson, GOC
Great Britain, was visiting the Northern Command.

In addition the Division was carrying out tactical training and the
Learners turned out and acted as umpires and generally got sworn at by
everyone.

To wind up the course, I was attached to the DADOS, APM and
Divisional Signal Company as well as the Divisional Gas Officer.

As to sport, Retford possessed a tennis club and we used to play there
every day. I also had some tennis at General Ross's house and Welbeck.
On one occasion I got up a team to play the 208th Infantry Brigade at
Welbeck. Our team was as follows:– General Ross and Major Tennant,
Colonel Clarke and Colonel Wallace, Major Smallwood and myself.

There were Divisional Sports and a dance was given by Mrs Ross. It was
during the time at the Division that I finally got my regular commission
papers signed after a great deal of trouble. General Ross kindly signed
them eventually.

Learners were always coming and going but the following were at the
Headquarters during the time that I was there:– Major Hon. D. A. Forbes,
Captains C. L. T. Matheson, N. Gladstone, C. Middleton, Lanigan O'Keefe,
Wyld, Thomson, R. G. Tudor, and Lieutenant Blair.

---

1. Probably Lieutenant J. M. Muir, the former commander of No. 5 Platoon, 'B' Company,
21st OCB.

Taking it all round I thoroughly enjoyed the course and I think I learnt quite a lot especially when I was with the artillery. Some people complain that they have nothing to do on these courses and that the actual staff officers take no notice of the Learner. Certainly this did not apply to me because I always found plenty to do, if only writing notes, and the staff without exception were always willing to tell you what they could, to help you.

Secondly it was a great change getting away from the parades and almost a relief. One imagined one was 'it' driving about in a divisional car.

After leaving Retford [on 28 August 1918], I went home on a few days' leave and then back to dear old Ireland and the dear old Reserve Battalion after an absence of three whole months.

69th (East Anglian) Division

GOC	Major-General C. Ross, CB, DSO
ADC	Captain W. B. Rodger, Ayr Yeomanry
Camp Commandant	Captain J. Bell, Ayr Yeomanry
GSO 1st Grade	Lieutenant-Colonel A. L. C. Clarke, DSO, A&SH
GSO 2nd Grade	Major K. Henderson, DSO, 39th [Garwhal] Rifles
GSO 3rd Grade	Captain C. H. Hart-Davis, E. Kent Yeomanry
AA&QMG	Lieutenant-Colonel A. W. B. Wallace, DLI
DAAG	Major R. J. K. Mott, MC, General List
DAQMG	Major W. Moore, London Regiment
APM	Captain S. Maples, Durham Light Infantry
DADOS	Major H. F. Weller, RAOC
ADMS	Lieutenant Colonel E. V. Gostling, DSO
DADMS	Major Taylor, RAMC
DADVS	Major D. R. C. Tennant, RAVC
Remount Officer	Captain Morris
Salvage Officer	Major Payne
Court Martial Officer	Major Harris
Signals	Major Smallwood, MC

13.

Back to the 3rd Argylls

———✦———

Weir was posted back to the 3rd Argylls at Kinsale in early September 1918 and, apart from a fortnight's stint as an assistant to the brigade-major at Cork, remained there for the remaining two months of the war.

When it eventually came, the German collapse on the Western Front was sudden; but it was hard to predict in mid-September when the Allies, still making piecemeal advances, had merely recaptured all the ground lost since March. Encouraged by the success of these limited offensives, however, Foch ordered an orchestrated assault in the West for the first time since April 1917. What materialized was an American-led offensive in the Meuse–Argonne sector, starting on 26 September; an attack by the British First and Third Armies towards Cambrai on the 27th; one by the Belgians and the British in Flanders on the 28th; and an offensive by the British Fourth Army, with American and French support, towards Busigny on the 29th. By now the Allies had some 217 divisions against the Germans' 197, though by Allied estimates fewer than fifty of the latter were fully fit for action. Collectively the general offensive would be the largest – and most decisive – battle of the war.[1]

The results were varied: the Meuse–Argonne operation was quickly brought to a standstill (partly because Pershing had chosen to advance through a broken country of forests and ravines, enfiladed from both flanks by artillery). Elsewhere, however, the attacks went well. By far the most successful was the one made by Rawlinson's Fourth Army at St-Quentin on 29 September that managed to break right through the Hindenburg Line and its reserve positions. Thereafter the advance slowed, but by 5 October the British were through the last defences and into unfortified ground.

By now Ludendorff had suffered a nervous breakdown and had decided to press for an armistice. What finished the Germans, apart from their own errors, was a combination of American numbers and Anglo-French combat effectiveness. Both British and Dominion forces applied a combination of technology and tactics that had come on in leaps and bounds since the Somme. Tanks played their part, as did the planes of the RAF. But the single

———

1. Stevenson, *1914–1918*, p. 429.

most important technological contribution to British success remained artillery. The Ministry of Munitions delivered a third more guns and howitzers (10,700) to the BEF in 1918 than it had a year earlier (6,500). These guns had more high explosive shells than they could fire, and many more gas shells than ever before (accounting for up to 50 per cent of the munitions fired in British bombardments). Also, the BEF had become expert at locating enemy batteries by aerial reconnaissance, flash spotting and sound ranging (using microphones that located guns from the 'air ripples' generated when they were fired). At Amiens, 95 per cent of German gun positions were identified before the battle began.[1]

On 4 October, the new German government (led by Prince Max of Baden as Chancellor) requested a ceasefire and a negotiated settlement based on Woodrow Wilson's peace programme (the 'Fourteen Points'). From 4 to 23 October, Berlin and Washington sent notes back and forth discussing the terms of the armistice. When Ludendorff tried to intervene, on 26 October, the Kaiser sacked him.

In Britain (and in Haig's HQ in France) the mood was favourable. Haig feared that without an armistice the Germans would retreat to the Rhine and hold it through the winter, while his own army was handicapped by manpower shortages and growing logistical difficulties. Henry Wilson, the Chief of the Imperial General Staff (and Haig's boss in London), estimated that by 1919 the BEF's divisions would fall from 59 to 44 or even 39, increasing the influence of the French Army on the battlefield and the French government at the peace conference. Britain, according to Jan Smuts (a member of the Imperial War Cabinet), was at its maximum strength and postponing a ceasefire into 1919 would mean 'an American peace', as well as threatening a Bolshevik takeover in Germany. Ministers believed the Fourteen Points were acceptable if Britain could achieve its own interpretation of them, and British public opinion seemed mostly willing to settle now. On 26 October the Cabinet summed up by favouring 'a good peace if that is now attainable', leaving Lloyd George to negotiate with a virtually free hand. The Paris conference of 29 October to 4 November decided on the German ceasefire terms and brought the European Allies into the Berlin–Washington consensus.[2]

What had begun as damage-limitation for Germany, in the hope of preserving at least some of its territorial gains and safeguarding its political system, ended by protecting it neither from defeat nor revolution. One of the key factors was the continuing Allied advance. More than half a million soldiers were killed or wounded during the weeks of armistice negotiation. Most of them, including the war poet Wilfred Owen, fell on the Western

---

1. Ibid., pp. 446-7.
2. Ibid., pp. 447–8.

Front. And yet the co-ordinated Allied assault was, by mid-October, bogged down in the Meuse–Argonne and in Flanders; the Canadians were held after crossing the Canal du Nord; and although the British Fourth Army had pierced the main Hindenburg Line defences on 29 September it took another week to clear the rear areas.[1]

From here on, however, the BEF faced only improvised positions. Against the line of the River Selle it fired 127 million pounds of shells from 1,320 guns before breaking through on 17 October. On 23 and 24 October the Flanders advance resumed; on 4 November, after another huge bombardment, British forces forded the Sambre and Oise Canal. From this point on, heavy fighting ceased on the British front and the Germans were in general retreat.[2]

The end was hastened by mutiny and revolution that began at the German port of Kiel on 4 November. Within days, most of the provincial capitals were in revolutionary hands and the tide was lapping around Berlin. On 9 November, Kaiser Wilhelm II abdicated and the socialist leader Friedrich Ebert became Chancellor. Next day Ebert agreed to Foch's armistice conditions, and the guns finally fell silent at 11 a.m., 11 November 1918.

The news must have been bittersweet for wounded veterans like Weir who had tried and failed to rejoin their battalions. Did he feel, however irrationally, that he had let his former comrades down? It's possible that he did. Certainly his diary entry for 11 November is understated, but that may be typical. It was, he wrote, a 'day to be remembered'. He added: 'We received the news of the Armistice at about 12:20 [p.m.] and the Band turned out and played the National Anthem and popular national airs. After that everybody or nearly everybody celebrated in the accustomed fashion and most of the Battalion were in bed at 5 p.m.'

Shortly after the Armistice, Weir returned to Brigade Headquarters in Cork to take up a new staff post as Education Officer for those soldiers about to be demobilized. One letter he received during this period, from Captain Stevenson, gives an intriguing glimpse of the revolutionary movement in Germany. Stevenson was still on the staff of 9th (Scottish) Division, one of the formations selected to form part of the British Army of Occupation. It had crossed into Germany in early December 1918 and set up its headquarters in Cologne. There it was met by a 'Soldiers' [and] Workmen's Council' – one of many that had sprung up all over Germany – and 'asked exactly what authority they might expect to retain'. When the members of the council were told 'none', recalled Stevenson, they 'withdrew hurriedly assuring us of their earnest cooperation'.

---

1. Stevenson, *1914–1918*, pp. 481–2.
2. Ibid., p. 482.

War Diary   September 1918–January 1919

So, after a few well-deserved days leave, I returned once more to my Reserve Battalion, the 3rd Battalion, who were still stationed at Kinsale. This time I had more luck and was not held up in Cork, as I had been when I first reported.

I was again billeted in Charles Fort and promptly put in command of 'B' Company, which was now entirely a Recruit Company.

Life went on just the same but luckily the captains and other officers had more work to do, especially field work and preparing for the weekly field practices on the rifle range at Preghane.

After I had been at Kinsale a fortnight I was ordered to Cork in order to undergo an Area Gas Course which lasted a week. Whilst on the course I lived at the Victoria Hotel. At the end of the course we were all given a written and oral exam and I received a good report recommending me for a further course at Dublin.

Instead of returning to Kinsale at the end of the week, I reported at the Headquarters No. 4 Sub-District as the Brigade Commander wished me to understudy the Brigade-Major, Captain R. W. Leach, Suffolk Regiment. As a matter of fact Leach had spoken to me about the matter one day when I met him in the Club and I was only too willing to take a job in Cork. Colonel Gordon was rather annoyed about it as he thought that the Brigade were hanging on to all his officers.

The work was interesting and I found plenty to do as the papers and files were in a chaotic condition and I was kept well employed in putting them into order. The sub-district was a large one and contained men of all arms and the numbers were considerably over those of a Brigade. There was plenty of secret and intelligence work and the Brigade-Major had a regular bevy of underlings.

However, after I had been there a fortnight, Colonel Gordon spoke to the Brigadier saying that he was very short of captains in the Battalion so I was sent back to Kinsale. I was rather annoyed at this for two reasons. The first because I had just got into my new job and the second because I knew what I should do at Kinsale.

The day I went back, the sub-district sports were held in Cork and I am glad to say that the Argylls carried off most of the events. I was on the Sports Committee.

As soon as I got back, I was again given command of 'B' Company. In addition to that I was elected on to the Mess Committee and also put in charge of the Entertainment Committee. The two latter kept me well employed. In the first place I was the senior officer in the Mess on the Mess Committee so I had to deal with plenty of frivolous complaints.

In the Entertainment line, I was kept busy with the band concerts that were to be given in Kinsale and at the Palace Theatre, Cork. In these two concerts we made about £120 which went to the Regimental War Fund for assisting men in the Regiment after the war.

I also got up weekly concerts which were given by the King's Jesters, the KOYLI Pierrots, The Smart Set Pierrots and the Officers. Other excitements took the form of a large Red Cross fête at Castle Bernard, Bandon and the Armistice celebrations in Kinsale.

November 11th was a day to be remembered. We received the news of the Armistice at about 12:20 and the Band turned out and played the National Anthem and popular national airs. After that everybody or nearly everybody celebrated in the accustomed fashion and most of the Battalion were in bed at 5:00. The few left enjoyed a good dinner in the Mess to the accompaniment of the Pipers and Band.

It took some time to settle down after the Armistice and very soon after I was recalled to the Sub-District at Cork to start the new Educational Scheme in the Brigade.

This time the Colonel offered no objections to my leaving but at the same time I was not keen on taking on the job after my last experience. In addition I knew nothing about Education or educating people. However I was told that did not matter.

As a matter of fact all one required was some method of organising the various classes, courses of instruction and to draw up general guiding rules for the various units.

Education work in Ireland was no sinecure. The Irish were unwilling to lend or even hire us their well-equipped Technical Schools. In fact we could not rely on the local authorities for any help.

The Scheme took some time to get going. Teachers were scarce owing to the fact that Group 43 was one of the first Groups to be demobilised. Officers would not take the Scheme to heart although education had practically taken the place of training. The men were unwilling learners and got bored with lectures very quickly. The Army authorities expected us to carry on without text books and stationery, absolute essentials.

But in spite of these difficulties we got going, firstly by making the Commanding Officers take up the Scheme and secondly by informing the men that Education had nothing to do with demobilisation and that if they took up subjects and courses it would make no difference to their leaving the Army.[1]

---

1. In other words, the Educational Scheme would not put back their demobilization. Most soldiers were desperate to return to civilian life.

I had a great deal of office work naturally, but I also spent time in visiting the various units and finding out the many difficulties that unit Education Officers had to contend with.

We also started Brigade Courses in Wireless and Electricity just to mention two things. And here my career as Brigade Educational Officer ends for I was ordered away on yet another job and again just as I had got a show into some kind of working order.

My stay in Cork this time was a pleasant one. First of all I was given my Christmas leave, ten days in all. This time I tried a different route from Ireland to my usual one and sailed direct from Cork to Fishguard on a Clyde boat.

Cork also managed to raise a Victory Ball in the Imperial Hotel and I was on the Committee. Dancing was becoming the craze and there were weekly dances at the hotel. The VADs also gave a dance.

What with dances and elections, Cork was a lively place. I lived at Moore's Hotel on the Quay but had most of my meals at the County Club.

The motor trips round the different units were also an amusing item. Ford cars were used and I think we had a breakdown every time we went out.

That is about all and thus ends my first experience of Ireland only to make me a confirmed Home Ruler in this troublesome country.[1]

From Captain W. S. Stevenson

HQ 15th Division,
British Army of Occupation,
near Cologne, Germany
5 January 1919

Dear Weary,

Good to have your address again – I was afraid I had lost you.

We're watching the Rhine all right, but from the E. bank and well into the middle of the country, about twenty miles from Cologne.

We had a great march up through Brussels and Liege, and altogether the advance from September 28th until our arrival here was a thing worth living through.

---

1. In May 1914, the Government of Ireland Act had been passed to provide self-government (Home Rule) for Ireland. But with the outbreak of war the implementation of the Act was postponed for twelve months, and subsequent events, including the Easter Rebellion of 1916, meant further postponements. It was finally superseded in 1920 by a new Government of Ireland Act that led, two years later, to Dominion status for the Irish Free State (effectively 'Southern Ireland') while the remaining six counties of Northern Ireland remained within the United Kingdom.

Now we are sitting still and I don't like it and wish I was well away from it all. Don't care for the people or the country or their beastly language, and in addition we have so much office work that it makes one irritable.

The best joke was the Soldiers' [and] Workmen's Council which flourished here and met us when we arrived. Asked exactly what authority they might expect to retain and we replied 'None.' They then withdrew hurriedly assuring us of their earnest co-operation.

Saw McQueen on leave in December. He was doing some Christmas shopping for the battalion. Also met General Kennedy who is at the Horse Guards. You meet all these people at the Caledonian Club which you ought to join if you are not already a member.

Saw French the other day, in fact spent part of New Year's Eve with him. Rather broke up his HQ I am afraid before we left in the early morning.

Can't quite remember where MacMillan is now. Rait had a letter from him from the Grosvenor Hotel. Mac's father died not very long ago. I think he is still with the 87th Brigade which the 10th [Argylls] are in, that is if he comes back to France.

Spoke to Colville on the phone when I was on leave. He was practically demobilized and had been back in his work in Motherwell for some months.

Bill Cunningham is still here also, commanding the Scottish Rifles, so there is still a remnant.

Write again – want to be demobilized but have no definite job to call me out.[1]

> *Ever yours,*
> *Staggers*

---

1. As the British Army still had many commitments after the end of the war – particularly in Germany, North Russia and in Imperial garrisons – demobilization of volunteers and conscripts was staggered. Men with scarce industrial skills (like miners) were allowed home first – hence Stevenson's remark about 'no definite job to call me out' – followed by the volunteers from 1914, 1915 and so on. The last to be released were the conscripts from 1918, though most were back in civilian life by late 1919.

14.

War Office

The war may have been over, but Weir's time in uniform still had more than a year to run. All of it was spent at the War Office in Whitehall, first as an attached officer on the staff of MOX, a sub-section of the Military Operations Directorate that was tasked with distributing secret telegrams; and later, with the disbandment of MOX pending, as a member of MO5, the Russian Section.

War Diary   January–March 1919

As I have already said, I had just got going at the Educational job, when I got orders to report to the War Office. I arrived there on January 15th and duly reported myself to MOX, Room 278. What is MOX? First of all it is a sub-section in the Military Operations Directorate, which is one of the three Directorates of the Imperial General Staff.

What does this mysterious MOX do? Nothing less than receive all the incoming secret telegrams into the War Office after they have been deciphered and distribute them to the Directors and Sections that take an interest in them.

But our job does not end there. We have to keep the other government departments such as the Foreign Office or India Office informed. We also distribute all telegrams received from these other offices, and despatch any telegrams that the General Staff Branches may require to be despatched.

Naturally one must know the War Office and its ways to carry out a job like this, and this is where the difficulty comes in. The War Office is totally different to anything else in the Army and it is necessary to start all over again.

Consequently one seems to drop nothing but a series of 'bricks' with unpleasant results. A new-comer on a job like this can only live and learn.

The work is hard and the hours fairly long – at least for office work. We usually work from 9:30 a.m. to 1 o'clock and from 2:30 p.m. to 6:45 p.m.

Each officer takes his turn to come early, that is at 8:45 a.m. but then he can leave at 5 o'clock so it is quite an advantage to do this.

He also takes his turn to do MO Orderly Officer and on this occasion he spends the night at the War Office.

There are two great disadvantages to a War Office job. The first is that it is purely office work and the second is that it is very hard to get any recreation. Also you have the expense of living in town, but this is met with the War Allowance of 10/– extra per day.

For the first few days, I stayed at 39 St Thomas' Mansions, but after I shifted into comfortable digs at 26 Chester Terrace with Davenport, who was at one time a Company Commander at the 21st Officer Cadet Battalion. He now fills an important and responsible position in the Staff Duties Directorate.

When I arrived in MOX, a Captain Cox of the Queen's was in charge, but he soon left and Captain A. L. Roche of the Royal Scots Fusiliers took over, whereupon he was made a General Staff Officer 3.

The other officer was Lieutenant C. R. Lighton of the 60th Rifles. Miss Mills, MBE, kept the registers and a record of the filing.

Towards the middle of February there were strong rumours that MOX was to be amalgamated to the corresponding sub-section in the Military Intelligence Directorate and this amalgamation took place on March 1st whereupon we left Room 278 and went up to 'Zeppelin Terrace'[1] to Room 5180.

The Military Intelligence and Information Agency (MIIa), or rather part of this large section, was run by Captain Hon O. S. Brett, OBE. He left on the amalgamation, but MOX had the addition of two MI Officers, Captain G. C. Lucas and Captain W. R. S. Mostyn, both of the Royal Fusiliers. Miss Haggard made an additional lady clerk. Thus the work increased, and so we carried on with three officers and two ladies.

From Major N. McQueen

10th Argylls, Germany
17 March 1919

My Dear Weir,

So glad to hear from you. I hope to be in town first week in April & will look out for you at the Caledonian Club. Of course you are eligible & if you want may use me to second or support. I am at your service.

Why don't you apply to come back to the Battalion? We should be delighted to see you. [Lieutenant-Colonel] Sotheby is on leave, you might

---

1. In October 1914, to accommodate the War Office's expanded wartime staff, temporary wooden offices were built on the roof of the Whitehall building and known unofficially as 'Zeppelin Terrace'. It was in one of these flimsy rooms that Weir worked from March to September 1919.

find him at Boodle's Club in St James's Street. Am awfully busy. Worse than when the war was on.

All news when we meet.

Yours,
McQueen

From **Major W. S. Stevenson**

HQ Lowland Division,
British Army of Occupation
Sunday 30 March 1919

Dear Weary,

I have been back here about a week, and find the whole show tremendously altered, even the famous old name of the Division [the 9th] having gone west.[1]

Perhaps there is no real hardship in that, as it is really no longer the 9th Division, only it rather hurts the feelings of one who has been so long with it as I have.

I met John Dashwood in the Caledonian Club. Doubtless you have too by now, as he appears to haunt the place at the moment.

The only bit of news I have, and that is only a rumour, is that John Kennedy is down to command the 10th [Argylls] out here. Whether he will really come or not I don't know, but he would do it really well as of yore, and it would suit him much better than going off to Aldershot when his present term of office is finished.

We are in the midst of farewell dinners here, but as most of the old members have joined since you left, they won't interest you. Incidentally speeches are made by various people who boast of their long service with the Division, consisting of anything from ten to eighteen months!

My love to Peirson, and tell him I'm sorry I didn't see him again. I was too busy with the Colonial Office.

Ever yours,
Staggers

War Diary

May–August 1919

At the end of May we were all cheered up by the fact that six weeks leave was open to us and it was decided that Lighton should go away on a fortnight first of all and then Roche go away for a month in July. My leave was to come in August.

---

1. In February 1919, the original units of the 9th (Scottish) Division were demobilized and replaced by others; the division itself was renamed the Lowland Division.

In order that the remaining ones should not be overworked during this time, we were given one additional officer. Thus Captain L. Welman, Middlesex Regiment, joined us.

Work seemed to increase instead of decrease, but the longer one remains, the quicker one gets at it.

However there is no doubt that the work is boring and cannot be called interesting for a person who is keen on regimental life.

As this is not supposed to be a treatise on work, I will switch off to the pleasure side of a life in town.

As I have already said recreation was almost out of the question and I was generally at a loose end on my days off.

During the first part of the summer I filled in the time by watching various tennis tournaments and went to Queen's, Chiswick and Surbiton. Sometimes I was lucky enough to get to a dance. Amongst those I went to were the War Workers at the Savoy, Lady Elizabeth Dawson's in Cadogan Square, Mrs Noel Harris' one at Hampden House [and] another at Lady Anstruther in Bruton Street.

Davenport and I sampled nearly every theatre and at one time we always went to a show once a week.

Other events included Henley Regatta, the Varsity Match at Lords, the Naval and Military Tournament at Olympia and I generally got a glimpse of the many marches and processions that seemed to be a weekly occurrence. There were one or two excitements in the office. The teas at one time were jolly, Roche got an MBE, while Lighton got engaged to be married. However to sum it all up, life in town and at the War Office doesn't suit me and I long to get away to the country or an occasional weekend at home.

As I write this I am still on the job and before I finish with the War House shall probably have some more to say. However I will now give a list of my superiors and fellow workers:–

Military Operations Directorate

DMO	Maj.-Gen. Sir P. P. de B. Radcliffe, KCMG, CB, DSO, RA, psc
DDMO	Brigadier-General W. M. St. G. Kirke, CB, CMG, DSO, RA
PA to DMO	Captain G. H. Batty, MBE
MOX	Captain K. T. Cox, R. W. Surrey Regt., until February 1919
	Captain A. L. Roche, MBE, Royal Scots Fusiliers
	Lieutenant C. R. Lighton, KRRC
	Captain N. A. C. Weir, Argyll & Sutherland Highlanders
	Captain G. C. Lucas, Royal Fusiliers, until May 1919
	Captain W. R. S. Mostyn, Royal Fusiliers, until May 1919
	Captain L. L. Welman, MC, Middlesex Regiment

      Miss Mills, MBE
      Miss Haggard
      Miss Wharmby
MIIa (when we amalgamated)
      Captain Hon O. S. Brett, OBE, Queen's Westminsters
      Captain G. C. Lucas
      Captain W. R. S. Mostyn
      Miss Balggallay
      Lady Sidney Mercer-Henderson
      Miss Kitston
      Miss Haggard

For all questions of administration we were directly under the Deputy Director of Military Operations.

Our clerks, with the exception of Corporal Brayton, our personal clerk, were furnished by MOD [Directorate of Military Operations] under Sergeant-Major Williams.

Our duties were to:-
    Circulate Operational and Intelligence telegrams
    Circulate Foreign Office, India Office and Admiralty telegrams
    Despatch Telegrams for the GS branches
    Keep a general index of all telegrams which concerned the GS
    branches and furnish copies of these telegrams.
On an average we deal with 170 telegrams a day.

15.

The Russian Civil War

Weir's last six months in uniform were spent on the staff of MO5, the War Office's Russian Operations Section. It was, in many ways, the most interesting period of his service, albeit without the comradeship (and danger) of his time in the trenches.

For much of the First World War, the Western Allies had shipped supplies to Russia through the ports of Arkhangelsk, Murmansk and Vladivostok. But since the Bolshevik Revolution of November 1917, and the withdrawal of Russia from the war the following spring, the erstwhile ally had become an ideological enemy. What prompted the Allies to intervene militarily was the Bolshevik attempt to prevent the Czech Legion (former soldiers of the Austro-Hungarian Army who had agreed to fight their imperial overlords in the cause of Czech independence) from sailing to Europe via the Siberian port of Vladivostok in the late spring of 1918. The Allies were also fearful that either the Bolsheviks or the Germans would capture the large quantities of supplies they had stockpiled in Arkhangelsk and Murmansk; and they hoped, if successful in defeating the Bolsheviks and restoring a Tsarist regime, to resurrect the Eastern Front against the Central Powers (particularly Germany).

So, in the summer of 1918, Britain and France (followed, soon after, by a further twelve powers including the United States and Japan) sent troops to support the anti-Bolshevik White Russian forces on various fronts in northern, eastern and southern Russia. The British alone sent 40,000 troops to the Arkhangelsk and Vladivostok regions, and for a time it seemed as if the intervention might be decisive as the White armies of Admiral Kolchak in Siberia, General Yudenich in the north-west and General Denikin in the south made steady inroads into Bolshevik territory. But one by one they were defeated: Kolchak was driven back from the Volga in the summer of 1919 (and later executed); Denikin was foiled in his attempt to take Moscow when he was defeated at Orel in October; and in the same month Yudenich failed to capture Petrograd (formerly St Petersburg) and sought refuge in Estonia where his army was disarmed and interned. Some White forces regrouped for a time in the Crimea, under General Wrangel, but by November 1920 they had fled in boats. By that time all Allied troops had been evacuated from Russia, bar the Japanese, who remained in northern Sakhalin island until 1925.

Weir played an active role (albeit from London) in the last six months of Britain's failed intervention in the Russian Civil War, and recalled the 'great attention' paid to events in Russia by Winston Churchill, by now Secretary of State for War (and a man he had last seen in the trenches of the Ypres Salient), who often came into MO5's office 'to study the map and the advances or withdrawals made'. Weir commented: 'He knew a great deal about the country and had a horror of Bolshevism.'

Weir's demobilization from the Army in early March 1920, a month after leaving MO5, coincided with the end of the Allied military intervention in Russia. 'It appeared to me at that time,' he wrote, 'that I had no earthly chance of getting a Regular Commission and that I had better get back to civilian life as soon as possible.' And so, reluctantly, he left the Army after five and a half years' service. He was still only twenty-four years old.

War Diary   September 1919

On my return from leave at the beginning of September I was surprised to find that MOX had not been disbanded. It was still on the go and various rumours as to its disbandment were current. Certainly there was urgent need for economy and it seemed that this section could almost be called a superfluous section as the work could so easily have been combined with that of C2 (Telegram) who as it was had to make certain distributions to 'A' & 'Q' branches.

On September 17th I received a polite note from the DMO saying that at a month from that date my services could be dispensed with. This came as a real shock as it meant demobilisation and I still had hopes of that Regular Commission.

From Colonel Walter Kirke   *Deputy Director of Military*
                                                 Operations, War Office
                                                 17 September 1919

In accordance with instructions which have been issued to effect a reduction in the strength of the MO Directorate, the following are warned that their appointments will probably cease by 15th October, 1919.

> *Captain N. A. C. Weir, Argyll & Sutherland Highlanders*
> *Lieutenant C. R. Lighton, KRRC*
> *Miss J. M. A. Mills.*

Miss P. Haggard.

Miss M. A. Wharmby

In making this notification, the DMO[1] wishes to express his thanks to the officers and ladies above mentioned for their loyal assistance during a difficult time.

W. Kirke

War Diary   September 1919–March 1920

Lighton then decided to leave the Army. Owing to his wound it appeared that he would have to leave sometime. He made this his opportunity to launch out into civilian life. We were ever so sorry to lose him and I felt sure that he would have been a tip-top soldier had he been able to remain on.

Meanwhile I ran round helter-skelter looking for another attached job in the War Office. It so happened that MO5 (Russian Operations Staff) wanted an attached officer at that time very badly as the existing officers had far more work than they could cope with. The DDMO agreed and I joined MO5b on September 18th.

MO5 dealt solely with operations in Russia and at this time it must be remembered that considerable controversy took place in Parliament and elsewhere as to whether our government were really justified in assisting the anti-Bolshevik forces against the Bolshevik forces. The Labour Party took the matter up very strongly as did also MPs like Colonel Malone, Colonel Wedgewood and Commander Kenworthy.

Certainly we were pouring supplies on the armies of Admiral Kolchak in Siberia, General Denikin in south Russia and General Yudenitch of the Russian North-West Army operating on the south of the Gulf of Finland. The Poles did not come our way much as they were helped by the French.

MO5 were then to carry out the War Office instructions which were received from the War Cabinet who were acting on the policy adopted by the Supreme War Council at Versailles.

The section under Colonel R. A. Steel, CMG, CIE, Indian Army, was divided into two sub-sections, A & B, under Major L. D. Heron, DSO, MC, Canadian Infantry, and Major D. J. Anderson, CMG, DSO, of the East Yorkshire Regiment.

Major Heron received the assistance of Captain E. H. Barker, DSO, MC, of the 60th Rifles, who was a GSO 3, and Major J. D. Deacon, MC, of the Gloucestershire Regiment.

---

1. Director of Military Operations, Major-General Sir Percy Radcliffe.

Major Anderson was assisted by Captain G. Peirson, DSO, MC, of the Durham Light Infantry, who was the GSO 3, and myself.

Lieutenant E. F. Chapman of the East Lancashire Regiment helped generally in keeping up the maps in the Cabinet room, S of S [Secretary of State's] room and certain other important people's rooms.

MO5a, dealt with South Russia and Siberia.

MO5b, dealt with North Russia and the Baltic States.

Barker looked after South Russia, Deacon after Siberia, Peirson on North Russia and myself on Baltic States.

North Russia soon came to an end and our troops there were successfully withdrawn by General Lord Rawlinson assisted by Generals Maynard and Ironside, who were both afterwards knighted. Peirson thus finished his job in November and left the Army, going out to farm in East Africa.

Yudenitch's North-West Army made a bold bid for Petrograd but owing to a lack of supplies the army withdrew being hotly pursued by the Bolo[1] so that soon his remnants were obliged to cross [into] Estonian Territory where they were immediately disarmed. Meanwhile the Estonians with Latvia, Lithuania and Finland assembled to discuss peace overtures.

Our mission was constantly changing here. General Gough was head for a time followed by General Haking, General Burt and General Turner. The German intrigues in the Courland caused considerable embarrassment to the Baltic States but eventually their forces were cleared out.

I remained with MO5b until the beginning of November when I was sent over to MO5a to take over Barker's job as he was about to proceed on a journey to South Russia with General Briggs. All of us were Old Wellingtonians, a curious coincidence.

General Denikin was then at the height of his successes, having just taken the town of Orel some 200 miles from Moscow. Our mission there under General Holman was doing good work. Unfortunately owing to the failure of Yudenitch and withdrawal of Kolchak in Siberia the Bolos were enabled to employ most of their forces against Denikin, with sad results to the latter, and after a slow retreat he finally lost all the ground he had gained since he resurrected the Volunteer Army. But this did not take place until the April of 1920.

While Barker was away I had a really interesting time. We were working in the main room of the section where our big map of Russia was placed.

The Secretary of State (Mr Winston Churchill) paid great attention to Russia and he would often come in to study the map and the advances or withdrawals made. He knew a great deal about the country and had a horror of Bolshevism. Naturally many notables accompanied him on these

---

1. Shorthand for 'Bolshevik Forces' or Red Army.

occasions and MPs were frequent visitors. Mrs Winston even came once. His Military Secretary, Sir Archibald Sinclair, Bart., was a keen follower of the situation. This was interesting from my point of view, as Winston and Archie Sinclair were Commanding Officer and second-in-command respectively of the 6th Royal Scots Fusiliers, our sister battalion in France.

Perhaps I should mention the visits of Colonel John Ward especially. He was a real honest soldier. The Army Council & Directors would also turn up in great force. Sir Henry Wilson always had an amusing story to tell to someone. It was our job then to show these personalities the maps and explain the results of the operations . . . a very interesting performance. The hours were longer than MOX. We rarely left before 7:00 p.m.

Heron was a great worker and it helped us to concentrate our attention on ours and not the gaiety outside.

This went on until Christmas then Barker returned so I drifted back to help Anderson in MO5b, I think Anderson is quite the brainiest soldier I have met.

The section had a severe loss when Heron left for a civilian job in January. His job was taken over by Major G. G. Waterhouse, MC, RE, who had just qualified at the Staff College. He had originally been in the section in its earliest stages. Major E. Clayton, OBE, RFA, also turned up once more after a long illness and thus Deacon went on leave. Chapman also left and I took over his jobs in addition to my own. This meant that I had to look after the maps. The one in the War Cabinet Room in the Prime Minister's house was the most exciting as I had chats with Lloyd George while I was working on it.

But lo and behold the pruning knife was at work again and the Russian Operations Section were asked to reduce. This was no doubt owing to the dreadful reverses that the anti-Bolshevik armies were undergoing. Kolchak and Denikin were now in full retreat, there was no North-West Army. The Baltic States were on the verge of making peace and Poland was inactive.

And we could not count the remnants at Archangel and Murmansk. And this brought us to the end of February when I considered it my duty to leave the Army. It appeared to me at that time that I had no earthly chance of getting a Regular Commission and that I had better get back to civilian life as soon as possible.

In any case they intended to disband MO5 on March 30th and amalgamate them with the Russian Intelligence people MIR.

The Colonel very kindly recommended me for a month's leave and it was granted so I proceeded on leave on February 6th.

Just before that auspicious event we had all changed our rooms. The Colonel and Anderson now shared a room while MO5 went up to the

4th Floor. This was owing to the fact that GHQ Home Forces had been disbanded and their remnants amalgamated with MO4 making it a very large section.

And I should have mentioned that old MOX had joined forces with C2 and so disappeared. This took place before Christmas. Roche and Welman stayed on for a short time to put C2 straight. They both then joined their units. Miss Haggard and Miss Wharmby, the sole surviving ladies joined C2.

My time off was spent mostly in going to theatres with Davenport. We had no games, except two days at golf, one at Neasden and one at Wimbledon.

The Caledonian Club was enlarged by taking over the Bishop of London's house next door and so it was quite comfortable.

Mother and Dorothy spent Christmas in town at Hughie's [Dr Hugh Haywood Weir] and we did more theatres. The Clarkes were also often up.

There were no private dances but I went to Ciro's, Rector's and the Portman Rooms.

We also had a Cadet Battalion Reunion at Prince's early in January. A good many old 21st instructors turned up and we had a merry evening. Goodness knows where we ended up.

I managed to get down to the Hunt Ball in Worcester and also to a dance given at the Guildhall by Mrs Britten.

* * *

And so I came back on March 1st at the termination of my leave. I reported at the War Office and was demobilised at Knaresborough House, Earls Court. And then being civilian once more went back home.

From **Brigadier-General Walter Kirke**

DDMO, War Office,
Whitehall, S.W.1
2 March 1920

My Dear Weir,
    Many thanks for your letter. I was sorry not to wish you good luck before you went, but do so now.
    You ought to get a good start with poultry[1] during the next two years. I keep chickens myself in a small way, and find it very interesting.
    The 'great thing' is to start with best stock. I got mine from Barrons. Let me know how you get on, and if I can be of any assistance to you.
                    Yours sincerely,
                    W. Kirke

---

1. Weir had decided to buy a poultry farm in Somerset.

War Diary   March 1920

Taking it all round I did not enjoy life in London at the War Office. The work was important and from a mercenary point of view the most paying I had had. But office life did not agree with me and it was only owing to the fact that I was working with pleasant people that I endured it. I owe a great deal to General Kirke, Colonel Steel, Anderson and old Roche and I met some of my best friends there, but still I enjoyed the regimental and training life much better.

I must not grouse. I should consider myself lucky to have that experience. It might serve me a good turn one day.

THE LAST WORD . . . FINALE . . . 1920

And so on March 1st 1920, I ended my Army experience and this diary must close.

My service extended from the 26th of August, 1914 to the 1st of March 1920. And what a multitude of experiences! A Platoon Commander, Specialist, Company Commander, Instructor, Staff Learner, Education Officer and War Office. Stationed with a Battalion, Brigade, Division and Whitehall. I cannot grumble at the variety. Working with the best of Commanding Officers, Platoon Officers, Non Commissioned Officers and men, I consider that it has been my good fortune to learn more in these few years than I should learn in a lifetime. I owe a great deal to the Army and especially the making of friends. Let me hope that I shall have the opportunity of meeting most of them again.

My two greatest blows were that I did not get my regular commission and that I did not get any war honours. Neither of these are my own fault, but one feels it.

To end let me give thanks to Almighty God for preserving me in all times and say:

GOD SAVE THE KING!

Postscript

After leaving the army, Weir became first a poultry farmer in Somerset, and then an official in the Colonial Office, working mainly in West Africa, where he ended his career as Chief Commissioner of the Gambia. In 1930 he married Hermine ('Jill') Fyffe, the daughter of the Rector of Holford, Somerset, who was thirteen years his junior. They had two children: Christina (b. 1934) and Celia (Mike Burns's mother, b. 1937). Weir died, at the age of seventy-two, in 1967.

Appendix

Final Farewells

10th (Service) Battalion, The Argyll and Sutherland Highlanders

Special Order of the Day

Farewell Addresses on Disbandment of the 10th (Service) Battalion, Argyll & Sutherland Highlanders after five years' Active Service Catterick Camp, Yorkshire, 1 November 1919.

From HRH Princess Louise, Duchess of Argyll

Colonel-in-Chief of the Regiment
27 October 1919

Dear Colonel Sotheby,

I understand that the 10th Battalion of my Regiment which you have so ably commanded for the past three years, is about to be demobilized.

I much regret that I am unable to have the great pleasure of inspecting your Battalion before it is demobilized and therefore ask you to convey my sincere appreciation of their splendid services.

I have, as you are aware, always taken the greatest interest in the career of the Battalion since it was raised, and am fully cognisant and justly proud of its glorious record of service. It has always maintained during the War, and since the fighting ceased, the highest standard and traditions of my Regiment.

The time has now come when it has to be disbanded, and I desire every member of the Battalion to carry with him into civil life, my heartfelt wishes for happiness, and prosperity in his new call in life. I feel confident that they will never forget their old Regiment, and continue to further its interests, and maintain its high traditions wherever they may be.

> *Believe me,*
> *Yours sincerely,*
> *Louise*

From Major-General Sir David Campbell, KCB
Commanding the Highland Division

Before your Battalion is finally broken up, I wish to convey to all ranks my great appreciation of the way in which, whilst forming part of the Highland Division, they have upheld the great reputation made by the Argyll & Sutherland Highlanders.

I am sure that every Officer, NCO, and man will look back with pride and satisfaction on the noble way in which he has lived up to the great traditions of a Regiment which has no superior in the British Army.

I am sure every man on his return to civil life will play the game in the future as he has in the past, and will always put his Country before his own selfish interests.

I thank you for what you have done, and wish you all goodbye and good luck.

From Brigadier-General J. Campbell, CB, CMG, DSO
Commanding 1st Highland Brigade

On giving up the Command of the 1st Highland Brigade, the Brigadier-General Commanding wishes to thank all ranks for the loyal manner in which they have always supported him, for their fine discipline, devotion to duty and steady conduct.

He has indeed been proud to command so fine a Brigade, and, although not put to the test of War as a Brigade, he always felt confident that all ranks would bring any operation that might be entrusted to the Brigade to a successful conclusion.

The Brigadier-General trusts that the esprit de corps and comradeship throughout the Brigade, which has been a most marked characteristic, will not be allowed to lapse. He hopes that when Officers and Other Ranks return to civilian life or go to other units they will never forget that each of them individually had a share in bringing the 1st Highland Brigade to the high standard it attained, and that each individual will maintain that standard whatever he may be.

The Brigadier-General wishes all ranks the best of luck in the future and hopes that they will look back in pride and pleasure, as he assuredly always will, to their period of service with the 1st Highland Brigade.

From **Lt.-Col. A. F. Mackenzie** *to* **OC 10th Argylls**   *Telegram*

Deeply regret disbandment of our Battalion. It leaves behind a record second to none on Balaclava Day.[1] I wish all ranks success, and I look back with deep pride to my Command, made so easy by all ranks, playing the game as they did. I wish you goodbye. Impress 10th Watchword, 'KING AND COUNTRY.'

From **Colonel John Kennedy, CMG, DSO**

formerly Commanding the Battalion

I regret very much to hear that my old Battalion is at length to be disbanded, but I cannot but feel glad to think that their history is to end with the termination of the War.

   I should like to repeat what I said once before, and this is, that there are no distinctions among the comrades of the 10th Argylls when they are off parade, so that, when they dismiss from their last parade, I cease to be their General, and shall be glad if they will call me Friend.

   I ask you to carry away with you this little bit of spirit of the old Battalion, so that its glorious traditions and influences may inspire and guide you in the future.

   A Battalion like the 10th is so much more than just a Regiment. It had a soul which inspired us all, and the memory of men like our old friends, Peter Bonnyman, Alex Maclennan, and many others must surely make us pause before the mean and despicable things of this world, and remember that some day we shall meet those great hearts, and they will probably know us as we are.

   God bless you all, and the cause for which we fought. If that was ever to be betrayed, all that is left of the 10th Argylls will rally to defend it once again.

From **Lt.-Col. W. J. B. Tweedie**

formerly Commanding the Battalion

Lt.-Col. Tweedie sends greetings to his comrades of all ranks in the 10th Battalion and wishes them the best of everything. He well knows that the esprit de corps which always distinguished the Battalion will continue to exist, although the 10th Battalion may officially cease.

---

1. On 25 October 1854, during the Battle of Balaklava in the Crimea, the 93rd Highlanders (forerunners of the Argylls) beat off an attack by Russian cavalry in an action immortalized as the 'Thin Red Line'.

He would remind everyone that there is virtually always room in the regular battalions of the Argyll & Sutherland Highlanders for Scotsmen of good character and physique.

Farewell and good luck.

From Lt.-Col. H. G. Sotheby, DSO, MVO   *Commanding Officer*

Officers, NCOs and men of the 10th Battalion.

At length the time has come when the Battalion is to be disbanded. It is a sad moment for me to feel that I am bidding farewell to my comrades.

The fine fighting spirit and high standard of discipline shown by all ranks during these five years have made the Battalion what it is. You joined up for the War. The War is finished; your job is done, and you may well be proud of the results gained. Wherever the Battalion has been, it has crowned itself with glory both during the fighting and since the Armistice was signed.

Officers and men have come from other Battalions of the Regiment, and even from other Regiments, but they have played the game with fine military spirit; and both during the War and since the Armistice, each and all have done their share in upholding the traditions of the Battalion and Regiment to which we belong.

Gallantry as shown in the fighting in which the Battalion has taken part, has never been excelled.

It has been to me the highest honour to be privileged to command such a Battalion, and I thank you for the great loyalty you have shown to me at all times.

In bidding you farewell, I wish you every good luck in the future.

Battle Honours

Loos	25 September 1915
Longueval (Somme)	14 July 1916
Butte de Warlencourt	12 October 1916
Arras	9 & 23 April 1917
Ypres (Passchendaele)	12 October 1917
Houthulst Forest	8 March 1918
Parvillers	8 August 1918
Herleville	23 August 1918
Crossing of the Somme	5 September 1918
Holnon Wood	10 September 1918
St-Quentin (Hindenburg Line)	30 September–2 October 1918
Avesnes	8 November 1918

Index